Praise for *PLC-Powered Data Teams*

"For anyone who has ever sat throug[h] _____ then *PLC-Powered Data Teams* is for you. Fi_____ :hers and leaders dedicated to returning 'lear_____ pro- fessional learning communities. Patric[k]_____ .per- tise, so we can immediately improve _____ .... every day and elevate teaching and learning for years to come. A must-read."

—Weston Kieschnick, associate partner, International Center for Leadership in Education, and best-selling author of *Bold School* and *Breaking Bold*

"*PLC-Powered Data Teams* is a tapestry of the best thinking of educational leaders of our time, weaving a refreshingly practical approach to using data as information to employ a response to evidence of teaching . . . full of practitioner insights. The book left me thinking 'We can do this!'"

—Arlene Borner, classroom teacher, staff development specialist, adjunct professor in Teacher Education Department, Crown College

"Polly Patrick and Angela Peery are two of my very favorite instructional gurus. In this book they bring authenticity, focus, and urgency to the most important practice for teaching and learning: intentional educator collaboration around instruction. Polly and Angela tell it like it is. The data team process they describe in this book (and have coached for me professionally for the past ten years) is a game changer. In this book they provide insights into the nuances of making educator collaboration purposeful in order to improve student outcomes and enhance the efficiency of the team. Teaching is both an art and a science. Polly and Angela help to shed light on the evidence-based ways that teachers can collaborate to replicate success and amplify the impact of one another. This book is essential for anyone who wants to implement research-based practices and move their team toward collective teacher efficacy. Truly there is no path to that goal without the wisdom highlighted by Polly and Angela."

—Kourtney Ferrua, author of *PrincipalED: Navigating the Leadership Learning Curve*, 2019 Oregon Nationally Distinguished Principal, and practicing district administrator

"As a district leader of data in a large-majority minority urban school district, I understand the importance of using data to drive school improvement processes such as data-driven PLCs. Integrating data into the PLC process is often difficult for district- and school-based administrators. *PLC-Powered Data Teams* is a must-read for all who desire a step-by-step guide for effectively integrating data into their current practices or for those who are new to the process."

—Rebecca A. Braaten, director of data, research, and evaluation, DeKalb County School District, Georgia

"As someone who has supported the implementation of Data Teams in my own district and supported many schools and districts across the country to do the same; I can say this process has an incredibly positive impact on teacher and administrator collective

efficacy and, in turn, student achievement. It is the power of teachers and administrators to adjust resources, time, and instruction based on student evidence that truly makes the difference. In *PLC-Powered Data Teams*, Polly Patrick and Angela Peery have captured both the 'why' and 'how' of this very process. This book empowers educators to continue learning and growing themselves as they strive to support each other and improve the outcomes for their students."
—Kyra Donovan, associate partner, International Center for Leadership in Education, and coauthor of *Rigorous Curriculum Design, Second Edition*

"Every PLC runs the risk of losing its direction and stagnating, using the time to sync content delivery schedules or to update curriculum maps. *PLC-Powered Data Teams* not only identifies why PLCs stagnate, but also identifies steps to reenergize, redirect, and refresh PLCs through Data Teams. I can't wait to share it with my teams!"
—Jeanne-Marie Garay, EL and ELA teacher, Faribault High School, Faribault, Minnesota

"*PLC-Powered Data Teams* is a timely read for agents of positive change. This text provides the guidance and tools necessary to develop highly effective PLCs that make mindful, data-informed decisions about student learning and teaching."
—Heidi E. Anderson, executive director, Augsburg Fairview Academy, St. Louis Park, Minnesota

"This is a must-read for all educators who believe that student achievement and growth translates to productive, successful citizens in the future. *PLC-Powered Data Teams* is a must-have to root instructional decision making in student evidence. This resource also provides stories of in-the-field experiences. You will utilize this to not only structure your professional collaboration, but to keep it focused squarely on student evidence. The best educators build from what students tell us in their work. You will find Polly's and Angela's approach easy to read, follow, and implement!"
—Adam Drummond, associate partner, International Center for Leadership in Education, and author of *The Instructional Change Agent*

"This work speaks to the power of leveraging the efficacy of every member of the collaborative data team to improve student success. The authentic invitation to learn and think collaboratively about student performance data is the ultimate gesture of professionalism at its best! This guide is essential to ensuring that the invitation to collaborate leads to effective and intentional discussions designed to link teacher collaboration directly to instructional effectiveness and student success."
—Dr. Jill Hackett, associate superintendent, Topeka Public Schools, Topeka, Kansas

"*PLC-Powered Data Teams* not only discusses how to build the collaborative teams, but expresses how the collaboration and data teams impact teaching and learning. Polly Patrick and Angela Peery give practical insights from teachers and leaders in the trenches that have successfully done the real work in their schools."
—Rhonda Lloyd, assistant principal, Jordan Vocational High School College and Career Academy, Phenix City, Alabama

PLC-Powered Data Teams

A Guide to Effective Collaboration and Learning

Polly Patrick | Angela Peery

FOREWORD BY JOHN HATTIE

AFTERWORD BY TYRONE C. HOWARD

International Center for
Leadership in Education.

International Center for Leadership in Education, Inc.
1587 Route 146
Rexford, New York 12148
www.LeaderEd.com
info@LeaderEd.com

ISBN: 978-0-358-56839-1

Contents

To my all-time favorite learning team: Anna, Trevor, Owen, Reid, and Jackson. Your love of learning, curiosity, and joy of discovery inspire my passion for this work.

—Polly (aka Gigi)

As always, my support system for writing this book was my husband, Tim. He did the cooking, washed a lot of dishes, took the dogs on walks, and did so many other things while I wrote all day and all evening quite a few times. Thank you, Tim, for standing by me for all these years and all these manuscripts!

—Angela

Acknowledgments

We believe that by definition a book about collaboration should have a long list of acknowledgments! They fall into a few overlapping categories of people: those who have challenged us to think, those who have thought along with us as we did our work, those who have contributed directly to the content and writing of this book, and those who have supported us personally.

We have learned from seminal thought leaders over these years. John Hattie, Douglas Reeves, Bill Daggett, Robert Marzano, Michael Fullan, and the late Richard DuFour have led seminars and written books that have challenged and shaped our thinking. Those books have received many a coffee (and wine) stain!

So many within ICLE have contributed to the writing of this book. Linda Lucey, Kate Gagnon, Julie Kerr, and Kirby Sandmeyer have been invaluable and patient and have given great guidance. Pam Palmer first suggested that we write the book while redesigning the *PLC-Powered Data Teams* seminar. Adam Drummond, Kyra Donovan, Kristen Painter, Sue Gendron, Weston Kieschnick, and Meeting of Minds groups all contributed greatly to this work over time. Former colleagues from another organization, Lisa Cebelak and Juan Cordova, also greatly influenced our work. Colleagues who have spent time thinking and discussing these ideas can't all get mentioned here, but you all certainly deserve it!

We acknowledge the many contributors to this book; some contributed directly and others have thought along with us about this work in their own systems. St. Charles Parish, Louisiana; Sabine Parish, Louisiana; East Baton Rouge, Louisiana; Savannah-Chatham County Schools, Georgia; Orangeburg School District 4, South Carolina; Colleton County Schools, South Carolina; McMinnville, Oregon; Joliet, Illinois; LaGrange, Georgia; Minnetonka and Minneapolis, Minnesota; Sioux Falls, South Dakota; Minot, North Dakota; Topeka, Kansas; Warsaw, Indiana; Columbus,

Georgia; and East Gresham, Oregon. Individuals who contributed Insights from Colleagues provided on-the-ground, real-time voices to this work, and we are grateful for you—Heidi Anderson, Linda Bishop, James Bozeman, Ankhe Bradley, Robert Culp, Adam Drummond, Kourtney Ferrua, Vernicia Gee-Davis, Kathryn Girard, Kim Gordon, Jill Hackett, Randy Hardigree, Kimberly Miles, Alex Moen, Tricia Nagel, Ken Oertling, Lisa Patrick, Ajit Pethe, Theresa Rouse, Daniel Scott, Lindsay Trinrud, Brent Veninga, Matt Wallace, and Alton White.

We also do acknowledge the many teachers who have trusted us with your stories. We loved thinking with you as you learned to become more effective teams and to care for students and their success.

Polly's note on a personal level: I was diagnosed with acute leukemia during this project. At the time of this writing I'm in remission! In my treatment at Methodist Hospital, I have *learned* firsthand the need for good evidence, making plans based on evidence, adjusting plans based on assessments, feedback, and the power of a collaborative team. My oncologists and team of nurses validate everything that is in this book about the importance of effective collaboration; I am deeply grateful.

Family is central to my life and work. My grown children, Lance and Megan, offered feedback, encouragement, and love that enabled me to complete this project. Their spouses, Lisa and Abram, are stellar examples of loving support. My husband, Mark, deserves more than a trophy. He is not only caregiver, editor, and sounding board, but is my dispenser of hope and admiration that keeps me going. Love you all!

Angela's personal note: I would like to acknowledge the colleagues far and wide who, for almost two decades, have contributed to my thinking, starting with Angela Binkley, my Data Team leader from the 2002–2003 school year. Who knew that the work done as part of that team would truly change the trajectory of my life? As Polly and I finish this manuscript, in the midst of a global pandemic, I find myself relatively healthy and full of gratitude for the professional and personal relationships that continue to sustain me.

About the Authors

Polly Patrick, MS, and ICLE Senior Instructional and Leadership Consultant, loves activating learning in many groups—young students or adults, struggling learners or high achievers. Polly has taught in multiple areas of English language arts and social studies with students from grades 7 through 12. For 20 years she also taught college and graduate school education students to improve classroom instruction and school culture. Polly speaks at conferences and training opportunities. She has led professional learning in Visible Learning, brain-based learning, instruction and engagement, school culture for learning, collaborative work, assessment, grading and reporting, school improvement, social and emotional learning, and literacy. Her passion these days is coaching teachers, principals, and instructional coaches about making learning happen. Her published writing now focuses on effective instructional practices to impact student learning; topics include the importance of questioning, the power of feedback in the learning process, and effective collaborative work. Polly lives in Minnesota with her husband, Mark, and enjoys every opportunity to spend time with her grown children and young grandchildren.

    Angela Peery, EdD, has been an educator for 35 years. She has been a middle and high school English language arts teacher, high school administrator, instructional coach, turnaround specialist, instructor of undergraduate and graduate English and education courses, National Writing Project summer institute codirector, author, and consultant. She is the founder of Dr. Angela Peery Consulting LLC, an organization that offers literacy instruction audits and other consultation and presentation services. She is the author of 16 books, including the bestsellers *The Data Teams Experience* and *Writing Matters in Every Classroom*. Angela lives with her husband of 32 years, Tim, two dogs, and two cats in Beaufort, South Carolina, and enjoys spending time at home, boating in the local waters.

About the International Center for Leadership in Education

The International Center for Leadership in Education (ICLE), a division of Houghton Mifflin Harcourt, challenges, inspires, and equips leaders and teachers to prepare their students for lifelong success. At the heart of all we do is the proven philosophy that the entire system must be aligned around instructional excellence—rooted in rigor, relevance, and relationships—to ensure every student is prepared for a successful future.

Founded in 1991 by Dr. Bill Daggett, ICLE, through its team of thought leaders and consultants, partners with schools and districts to implement innovative practices to scale through professional learning opportunities guided by the cornerstones of our work: the Daggett System for Effective Instruction and the Rigor/Relevance Framework. Additionally, ICLE shares successful practices that have a positive impact on student learning through keynote presentations, the Model Schools Conference, and a rich collection of publications. Learn more at LeaderEd.com.

Foreword

Do I love data?

Of course, I love data. I have spent my academic career as a measurement, psychometrician, and statistical analyst. Give me a data set, and I am in heaven; I clean, play, manipulate, analyze, replay, and collect more data. My computer is stuffed with data. My book *Visible Learning* is based on 300 million students. I have analyzed census data, sports data, and even data from television quiz programs. Honestly, I do not think there is a number I have not captured, considered, and ultimately cherished.

But these data are building blocks. It is the interpretation of these data that matter most. And that is my passion—interpreting. I am continually curious about why something is happening or how something works. I use data to see if my thinking is right—or wrong—and to build models that explain patterns. To me, it is sad to see those who just stop at the raw numbers.

Consider students who think the work is over when they get a grade. Grades are indicators, and the key point is to interpret these indicators so that learning improves. Think of the doctoral students who think collecting the data is the core of their theses (it is not, it is their interpretations); think of the school leader who thinks data will insulate them from critique; think of the superintendent who has walls of fancy graphs. Schools are awash with data. Systems love to collect data. Politicians, like Scrooge McDuck, wallow in data, throw up numbers in the air, and bask in decimal points tumbling all around them.

The last thing many schools need is more data. Instead, we need more interpretation. We need to move conversation into action. We need more evaluative thinking about these data.

I am sure if we deleted over half the data schools collect, no one (but those who collect it) would notice. Or care.

The right question is, do we have the right data for the right question at the right moment and have we interpreted appropriately? This is where *PLC-Powered Data Teams* provides greatly needed tools and strategies. This book is about the collective interpretation of data in teams. Our impact as teachers is discovered through the triangulation of evidence—data, student voice, our impressions. But interpretation is the key. And more important is the triangulation of evidence *in collaboration with others.*

The collective efficacy of teachers is a powerful influence in school, especially when teachers work together to develop high expectations about what it means to impact students and what growth looks like. As important is questioning the cognitive biases we all have when interpreting evidence, particularly about our own impact. I, for example, have high levels of confirmation bias. I tend to believe that when I have positive impact, it is clearly my influence. But when there is a lower impact, I tend to think that it is obviously due to extraneous influences. Such rose-tinted glasses need to be questioned. Yes, they should be questioned in high-trust environments, but I am not doing my students any favors by not being questioned, hearing alternative views, and refocusing on improving the interpretations about data. As outlined throughout *PLC-Powered Data Teams*, this is a key function of data teams, and why Polly Patrick and Angela Peery pay so much attention to building efficacious teams.

Many educators roll their eyes when the word *data* is mentioned. Often, this is because data means test scores. But there is so much more data in our schools, such as data about what happens in the classroom, walk-through data, social and emotional data, data about what professional learning communities do and focus on, parent data, and teacher reflection data. It is this rich tapestry of data that needs interpreting, not merely test scores. Often the test score is an outcome of a long process. Understanding this process is the true essence of teaching.

I spend a lot of my time collecting data on how teachers and students learn. Often, though, we lack a developed language to articulate how we think through or identify the learning strategies we use. Learning is more of a staccato of ups and downs than a smooth linear process. And learning is invisible. It happens within the brain, and we thus cannot see it. These are all very real hurdles to understanding and unlocking the efficacy of learning. But if we are to improve—if we are to increase student success—we need to make our students' learning process visible. We must understand the misconceptions, the errors, the wrong turns that they are making, how they are thinking as they are solving problems, and how they are (or not) adjusting to their progress. Data help us do this, especially data that are analyzed and interpreted in teams.

The messages, the examples of the big ideas in action, and the focus on collectively interpreting data to help educators further enhance the learning lives of students—this is the gift you will receive reading *PLC-Powered Data Teams*.

John Hattie
University of Melbourne
Carlton, Victoria, Australia

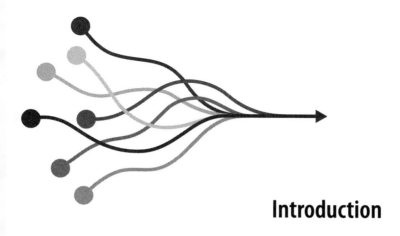

Introduction

A book about working together, written in the midst of a pandemic that's keeping us apart—who would ever have guessed that the two of these would come at the same time? However, the intersection of these two events turned into *PLC-Powered Data Teams: A Guide to Effective Collaboration and Learning* as a catalyst for some amazing learning. The COVID-19 pandemic has pushed many of us apart physically yet causes us to pull together more intentionally than ever. All over the world, people have had to leave school buildings and colleagues that they saw daily and may have spent years working with. Teachers may now realize more than ever that they need connection with others as they face truly uncharted waters ahead in the profession.

Prior to March 2020, indoor, face-to-face team meetings happened with great regularity all over the United States and beyond in school buildings. If it was 8:00 a.m. on Tuesday, the team met. Many of those meetings were simply examples of committees who spent a fixed amount of time filling out forms for efficiency and expediency but were actually short-circuiting instructional effectiveness. Not all teams were motivated to meet because they were improving student learning. After school buildings were closed and teachers and students were sent home to work and learn, many educators realized that they needed their teams to run differently.

Educators must all work in teams these days but are often unsure of how this contributes to student achievement. They attend meetings that hardly impact their daily instructional practices; they go through the motions but do not even monitor the impact of innovations put in place. *PLC-Powered Data Teams* aims to focus on the critical link between teacher collaboration and student success. The ultimate goal of the Data Teams experience is to support all learners—both teachers and students—through ongoing

1

innovation and reflection. Thus, this book is written to support teacher learning that then supports student learning.

PLC-Powered Data Teams seeks to capture the change that results when teams hit the refresh button. When the practices described in this book become a reality, the purpose of teams meeting together becomes more apparent. Teachers find themselves being stronger together than alone, intentionally and collaboratively planning lessons that make a difference, implementing innovations and tracking their success, and monitoring the learning that is right before them. All of these things become what is done in meetings—instead of filling out forms and checking off boxes for compliance.

Whether you have been on a team for years, are rebooting professional learning communities (PLCs), or just starting a Data Teams (DT) process, this book is for you. Our hope is that it becomes a catalyst for dialogue and a guide for the many possibilities you can enact. Our goal is that it provides you practical ways to initiate, refresh, tweak, or fully restructure practices. We also hope that it helps you reconnect with or renew your passion for collaboration and for seeing your students thrive.

PLC-Powered Data Teams: A Guide to Effective Collaboration and Learning can be the foundation for the following:

- Individual thinking,
- A book study by a group of teachers or leaders, and
- Ongoing growth after initial training in Data Teams.

Each chapter can be read and used as a stand-alone, or it can enhance the material in other chapters if several are read together. Briefly, each chapter is described below.

Chapter 1 focuses on what the actual work is and your own role in teaching, learning, and effective collaboration. This is a terrific chapter for anyone who wants to recharge their own passion about the work of being both an effective teacher and learner.

Chapter 2 distinguishes professional learning communities from professional committees. It also discusses what creates an effective team that is safe and welcoming for all teachers. Collective efficacy is described; many educators now know this to be the most effective factor in student achievement. The chapter concludes with a practical focus on the formation of teams.

Chapter 3 examines how to use existing data more effectively. It also discusses how to collect evidence of learning that allows students to achieve at higher levels.

Chapter 4 is about organizing and validating your prior knowledge with important historical origins and a research base for this work. Here we discuss not only aligning Data Teams work with standards, but also ensuring the interaction of that standard with instruction and assessment practices.

Chapter 5 provides the frame for Data Team meetings. Here we present a description of the roles of various members of the team, the components of meetings, and meeting cycles. This chapter is central to implementing the work and serves as a nuts and bolts guide.

Chapter 6 focuses on effective instruction. If you're not changing your instructional practices, then you're not really having Data Team meetings. In this chapter, we bring together instructional practices, the International Center for Leadership in Education quadrants, and teacher-student interactions. This chapter is meant to recalibrate your thinking about the significance of teacher-student interactions.

Chapter 7 discusses initiating Data Teams in addition to accountability and sustainability. The chapter presents what all of that looks like at the system, school, team, and student levels. The discussion is a catalyst for dialogue around how we both define and redefine accountability in our system. The chapter will conclude with multiple practical strategies and tips on sustaining this work even if your district has been at it for a long time already.

Each chapter includes features called Insights from Colleagues embedded in the narrative. We also include Questions to Consider at the end of each chapter.

PLC-Powered Data Teams: A Guide to Effective Collaboration and Learning is designed to support a culture of people working together and consistently tracking evidence of their success. PLCs and Data Teams are not simply another program or initiative; they should be the soul of how educators work. So, we invite you to think and reflect with us as you read these pages—then be ready to act in fresh, powerful ways.

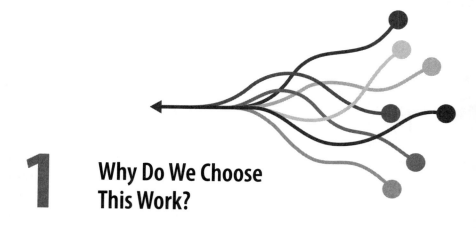

1 Why Do We Choose This Work?

Working hard for something we don't care about is called stress. Working hard for something we love is called passion.

—Simon Sinek, *Together Is Better*

"Stronger me's make stronger we's" was the slogan on the billboard along the highway. The slogan also summarizes this first chapter. As educators, all of our collaboration work comes back to what each individual brings to the table. Whether our focus is on students or teachers, the issue is gaining confidence built on growing competence to do what we choose to do (Figure 1.1). We effectively lead both teachers in our buildings and students in our classes as we first know ourselves.

Throughout this book, we focus on how educators grow their competence. In this chapter, we discuss two factors related to competence: personal mindsets and professional attitudes. Let's address personal mindsets first.

It's Personal

Simon Sinek (2011) reminds us in his work *Start with Why* that whether in business or in education, we too often start in the wrong place in what he calls the Golden Circle. He developed this model as he states, "People don't

FIGURE 1.1   We Grow in Our Confidence as We Grow in Our Competence to Be Able to Do What We Choose to Do

buy what you do, they buy why you do it" (Sinek, 2011, p. 41). He illustrates this point simply with three layers of circles, with the "why" in the center, the "how" in the next ring, and the "what" in the outermost ring.

Most fast-paced work goes right to the "what to do." From there, people often go to "how to get it done." The "why we do it" is in last place if it is discussed at all.

Recently, a board chair of a large radio station was being interviewed; he told the host that the focus of the organization was on what and how to do their work. That was to be their winning combination (MPR News Staff, 2020). Sinek's work reminds us that we need to reverse that and first identify why we're doing what we're doing.

In *Ten Mindframes for Leaders* (2021), John Hattie and Raymond Smith apply Sinek's model to the work of educators:

- The why—these are the beliefs and mindframes about our role as school leaders;
- The how—this is the set of high-probability practices drawn from research with effective implementation; and
- The what—these are the results that we create, the positive impact on student learning progress and achievement.

All three of these are consistent with our approach and the work we are discussing in this book.

We have all been in educational meetings where someone was talking from the what and how perspective. Where was your head during those meetings? Many people are in their to-do lists or other places in their minds. Can you also recall times when someone was speaking to you about their purpose with great passion? Where was your head then? Were you drawn in, ready to take action? Were you inspired? Which do you want for your own meetings or classrooms? Now, this is not the time to simply sit and feel bad about something, but rather to reflect and rekindle the passion that you hold for the work of education. Principal Heidi Anderson shares her experience.

Heidi's purpose drives her passion. Dr. John Hattie writes in *Visible Learning Insights* (2019), "Becoming a teacher is one thing; being a teacher and remaining a teacher is another" (p. 94). This is an oft-used saying. Why we do the hard work of being an educator is the place to start, and how we look at the work is also influenced by our current mindset.

INSIGHTS FROM COLLEAGUES
Heidi Anderson, principal, Minneapolis, Minnesota

As a teacher and educational leader, my why has always been about my students. After years of giving and spreading myself thin, I was unfocused and unhappy. Instead of spending my days putting out daily fires for students, I wanted to work to dismantle systems of oppression *with* my students. Students will always be my overarching framework. However, to sustain my work and give what I have, I needed to focus my why. I believe public education is a civil right. Education is the most valuable tool to dismantle racism and create a more equitable society; therefore, I work to provide a high-quality, culturally relevant, and restorative experience for all students. When I refocused my why, I became reinvigorated to make good, necessary trouble, as the late Representative John Lewis expressed it.

Carol Dweck (2017) has written extensively about how mindsets work. We may remember the words *fixed* and *growth* from her work. To summarize, a fixed mindset is one where a person's self-perception may be clouded by thinking they only have so much ability. They think they can't do certain things, or they hit proverbial walls and stop trying. Challenges appear as problems or obstacles. Lisa Trei gives us insight into Dweck and her work:

When psychology Professor Carol Dweck was a sixth-grader at P.S. 153 in Brooklyn, N.Y., she experienced something that made her want to understand why some people view intelligence as a fixed trait while others embrace it as a quality that can be developed and expanded.

Dweck's teacher that year, Mrs. Wilson, seated her students around the room according to their IQ. The girls and boys who didn't have the highest IQ in the class were not allowed to carry the flag during assembly or even wash the blackboard, Dweck said. "She let it be known that IQ for her was the ultimate measure of your intelligence and your character," she said. "So the students who had the best seats were always scared of taking another test and not being at the top anymore." (Trei, 2007)

For teachers, fixed mindset may be their thinking about that next observation, and for students, it may about their thinking about the next test. Either way, becoming more self-aware can help. A person operating with a growth mindset in a given situation sees a new problem as a challenge and an opportunity to learn. It is imperative to use the concept of mindset appropriately. After a long conversation with Carol Dweck, John Hattie (2017) said of her work, "She claimed that growth mindsets can inspire different goals, shape views about effort, but she has never claimed in her academic writings that there is a state of mind called 'growth mindset'—it is not an attribute of a person, it is a way of thinking in a particular circumstance. She has undertaken many research studies to understand when and where it can be invoked to lead to better outcomes. It is more a coping strategy than a state of being."

The graphic in Figure 1.2 can be used to support moving through to new levels of just this kind of coping. It allows common language to discuss mindset with adults for self-assessment to facilitate conversations with a colleague or students.

New learning—or even hard learning—keeps an individual using a growth mindset intrigued and moving forward. For each of us and our students, the word *yet* added to "I don't get this" can change perspective and mindset.

To be effective, teachers must use the concept of mindset appropriately. Hattie (2017) goes on in the same blog to give the appropriate uses of growth mindset.

The key question is, "*WHEN is the appropriate situation for thinking in a growth manner over a fixed manner?*" In these situations, having access to growth thinking helps resolve the situation, move the person

Moving from Fixed to Growth Mindset:

1. Enduring (Fixed Mindset): never—can't imagine thinking this way.
2. Gaining Awareness: Realizing it's possible to think this way.
3. Deciding: I want to approach things this way—and I will.
4. Learning: I'm reminding myself regularly and making progress.
5. Growing (Growth Mindset): This is becoming a more natural response—I'm enjoying it.

FIGURE 1.2   Mindset Progressions

forward, and not lead to resistance, over reaction and fear of flight into a fixed mindset. The major situations for growth mindset are:

- When we do not know an answer
- When we make error
- When we experience failure
- When we are anxious

In these situations, having a growth mindset is a most appropriate coping strategy.

Knowing how to use a growth mindset in those four situations can help administrators, teachers on teams, and students in the classroom. Clearly, we need to keep from using mindset as a label or set characteristic. Alex Moen is well equipped to illustrate the need for mindset in her work.

INSIGHTS FROM COLLEAGUES

Alex Moen, counselor and teacher, Augsburg Fairview Academy, Minneapolis, Minnesota

I work with students who face huge barriers to school success. As a result of broken systems, they've failed classes, scored poorly on tests, had conflicts with teachers, etc. My students come to our school after years of failure in the system; they don't believe in themselves. They have no sense of self-efficacy, and therefore no hope. If we have no hope and no belief in our own abilities, where is our curiosity? Our interest? Our internal motivation? How can we learn? My students come to our school with a fixed mindset; they believe if they don't know something or can't do something, they will never know it and never be able to do it. It is our most important job at our school to teach them a growth mindset: that we *all* can grow, and learn, and change—teachers and students.

As educators, we already know this; yet we often fail to remind our students of it. It is obvious to us! Of course, our students are always learning! That's the whole concept of education. For most of their lives, our students have received the message that they are not good enough. Every failing grade on their report card, every below-competency test score, every trip to the principal's office tells them they do not measure up. How many more times, then, do they need to hear the opposite? It needs to be woven into everything we do. As Polly says, the word *yet* is very powerful.

"I don't know how to do this."

"You don't know how to do this *yet*."

"I can't figure it out."

"You haven't figured it out *yet*."

Such a simple thing that educators take for granted, but it is the only thing that can unlock a student's desire to learn. And there is nothing more satisfying than seeing that tiny spark of belief alight in a student's eyes.

As Alex points out, the students are always learning. Every educator knows that students watch us and how we approach solving a problem or responding to a mistake. They learn as much from what we do and how we treat them as from what we say about the standard of the day. The effective use of mindset needs to be a core component of how we educators look at ourselves and our students.

Mindsets go beyond labels and shape the narrative and climate of classrooms and schools. In his profound book *The Innocent Classroom: Dismantling Racial Bias to Support Student of Color*, Alexs Pate (2020) speaks to the impact of a negative narrative: "I believe that negative narratives are internalized as guilt in the bodies of our children. And when this happens, the lingering innocence is stolen right out of their lives, maybe forever. They are trapped. We all are. We are all victims in this reality where the bad stories about us dictate how people see us" (p. 4). This is compelling motivation for us to first tend to our own thinking and then create communities that share that positive narrative we all need to learn.

Polly has often spoken of educators as "hope dispensers." What an opportunity we have. That is the power that the "me" brings to the "we"! Victoria Safford (2016) speaks to this in her poem "The Gates of Hope":

Our mission is to plant ourselves at the gates of Hope—
Not the prudent gates of Optimism,
Which are somewhat narrower.
Nor the stalwart, boring gates of Common Sense;
Nor the strident gates of Self-Righteousness,
Which creak on shrill and angry hinges
(People cannot hear us there; they cannot pass through)
Nor the cheerful, flimsy garden gate of "Everything is gonna' be all right,"

But a different, sometimes lonely place,
The place of truth-telling,
About your own soul first of all and its condition,
The place of resistance and defiance,
The piece of ground from which you see the world
Both as it is and as it could be
As it will be;
The place from which you glimpse not only struggle,
But the joy of the struggle
And we stand there, beckoning and calling,
Telling people what we are seeing
Asking people what they see.

Used with permission from the author

Where do personal passion and mindset intersect with professional attitudes? This hope is strategically part of successful classrooms. Randy Hardigree, a biology teacher in Georgia, shares important changes he made because he was challenged to grow.

INSIGHTS FROM COLLEAGUES

Randy Hardigree, biology teacher, LaGrange High School, LaGrange, Georgia

Several years ago, after being introduced to some new people and unfamiliar concepts, I began to question the way learning was happening in my "well-oiled" classroom. I have always taught with great passion, heart, and precision. Far into my career, I was thought of as an excellent and caring teacher. But when faced with the question, "Where is the thinking happening in your classroom?" I found myself bewildered. I came to the disturbing realization that I was the one doing all the thinking! Not a good feeling for me, as I have always wanted to do my job well and have put great energy into giving my students a quality learning experience.

I teach a high-stakes, compulsory course tethered to a state-mandated exam. The breadth of mandatory content is daunting, and the pressure we teachers feel is heavy. The thought of slowing down seemed like a death sentence; yet I felt compelled to do just that if I was going to catalyze a true shift. From my perspective, I was putting my students and myself at great risk by stepping outside my comfort zone, but I couldn't continue the way I had been and feel good about it. In hindsight, I think it would have been a much greater risk to maintain the status quo.

I don't take personal credit for any of the changes that have happened since then. I had the help of some amazing colleagues, mentors, and authors.

With a better understanding of personal mindsets, let us now turn our attention to the factor of professional attitudes.

It's Also Professional Beliefs

Just as Randy described to us moving from his comfort zone to new levels of his work, we must all look at our instructional practices and attitudes. As discussed earlier, John Hattie calls these *mindframes*.

Why examine our attitudes? There is the strong possibility that if teachers go to work and refuse to grow, then that is what students may do as well. Hattie's research is the international gold standard connecting student learning to teacher practices. Beyond the millions of students he has included in the studies and the thousands of meta-analyses that have been examined to record roughly 200 factors that impact student learning, Hattie has proposed ten mindframes that will make any teacher more effective when helping students learn. "Remember, success is based not only on competencies, but more on mindframes; less on what we do and more on how we think about what we do" (Hattie and Zierer, 2018, p. 160). As you examine the ten attitudes, take time to reflect on which of these you already fully embrace, which you want to tweak or increase your ownership of, and which you challenge yourself to add anew to your practice.

1. I am an evaluator of my impact on student learning.
2. I see assessment as informing my impact and next steps.
3. I collaborate with my peers and my students about my conceptions of progress and my impact.
4. I am a change agent and believe all students can improve.
5. I strive for challenge and not merely "doing your best."
6. I give and help students understand feedback and I interpret and act on feedback given to me.
7. I engage as much in dialogue as monologue.

8. I explicitly inform students what successful impact looks like from the outset.
9. I build relationships and trust so that learning can occur in a place where it is safe to make mistakes and learn from others.
10. I focus on learning and the language of learning. (Hattie and Zierer, 2018, p. xv)

These are powerful attitudes for us to consider and study. Let's just take a brief look at each of the ten in practical terms to further prompt our thinking.

I Am an Evaluator of My Impact on Student Learning

This can be described as the teacher being the GPS of a classroom. Most of us depend on a GPS in our cars or phones to get us to our destination. We should apply the analogy to our teaching, asking, "How reliable was I in getting students to their destination of learning in today's lesson?" Teachers need to know if their practices paid off every day. If not, they need to know how to plan next steps in response. This type of self-evaluation is especially critical as schools navigate remote and hybrid instruction. These more recent platforms call for us to remember the evidence of the cause-and-effect impact of our teaching on our individual student's success in achievement. See Chapter 6 for further development of these effects.

I See Assessment as Informing My Impact and Next Steps

Have you ever heard your GPS say, "Recalculating"? As a GPS, every teacher needs to use all forms of assessment to determine when and how to do the routing for the entire class and for the individuals within. Chapter 3 examines how to do this in more depth. However, teachers need to know their students, listen to what they say, watch what they do, and strategically collect evidence of learning.

I Collaborate with My Peers and My Students About My Conceptions of Progress and My Impact

Collaboration in the service of collective efficacy is the purpose of our PLCs (professional learning communities). We need to take that collaborative stance into our classroom as well. Ask yourself, "What am I like as a collaborator?" Feedback given and received can invite learning, teamwork, and a focus on student achievement.

I Am a Change Agent and Believe All Students Can Improve

As Bob Johansen (2012) in *Leaders Make the Future* puts it, "We need to have the ability to turn dilemmas—which unlike problems, cannot be solved—into advantages and opportunities" (p. 55). He goes on to say we must be able to "put together a viable strategy when faced with a challenge that cannot be solved in traditional ways" (p. 59). Educators must become adept at "dilemma flipping" which, in turn, makes them more effective change agents. If there is nothing the coronavirus has taught us, it is this—we must learn to use dilemmas for opportunities to change.

I Strive for Challenge and Not Merely "Doing Your Best"

"Do your best," often said by teachers, leaves so much room for learners (colleagues and students) to not push themselves. They may think they only need to give whatever they have given previously as their best. For example, if a student has been given credit for merely putting his name on paper in a class before and later runs into a teacher who expects far more, he will be confused. He thought he was "doing his best" before because he received full credit for very little effort. We all want to do just a bit more than we have done before. Is that the challenge we give ourselves and others with whom we work? How do you urge both your colleagues and students to give more than they have previously?

I Give and Help Students Understand Feedback and I Interpret and Act on Feedback Given to Me

Effective feedback is sometimes called "feed-forward" because of its power to guide learners toward mastery. Vague praise like "good job" is not productive and is the equivalent to someone's answer of "fine" when you ask how they are. Return to the GPS analogy. We often receive updates from a GPS while driving about how far we have to go. In the same way, educators need to give feedback that helps learners find themselves between where they are, what they know now, and what they still need to learn to get to mastery.

Similarly, when our colleagues provide us feedback in a collaborative meeting, or when they do so after observing us teach, we need to be ready to act on that feedback. What is the last piece of feedback that you received from a colleague? How did it feel to receive it? And, most importantly, what did you do differently as a result?

I Engage as Much in Dialogue as Monologue

The word *dialogue* is about a reciprocal conversation; in contrast, the word *monologue* clearly focuses upon the self. We must ask ourselves: Do we spend more time talking or listening? Do we draw others out and think together or predominantly give only our own perspectives, information, and directions? Most often whoever is doing the talking is doing the learning. Therefore, we must seek to do more listening and allow others—both colleagues and students—to engage in dialogue with us. We should strive for a more equitable back-and-forth.

I Explicitly Inform Students What Successful Impact Looks Like from the Outset

It is hard to be motivated if you don't know where you're going. Most likely you've not been on a trip without knowing the final destination. In cooking, it helps to know what the finished product looks like (this is why cookbooks and websites have photos). These are just two of the analogies connected to this mindframe. Let's apply them to the work of education. While we're working, we want to know if our thinking is leading in a direction that will help us solve a problem or flip that dilemma we discussed earlier. For example, if we have certain students who continue to struggle with a basic concept that they need to master before moving on to new learning, we must find ways to reach them and push them. Dialogue with our Data Team colleagues helps us clarify both the expected end result and the path there.

I Build Relationships and Trust So Learning Can Occur in a Place Where It Is Safe to Make Mistakes and Learn from Others

Earlier in this chapter we examined mindset and how central it is to learning. Whether we are in team meetings or in the classroom, relationships empower us to move learning forward; otherwise, broken relationships can become obstacles that keep people from learning. How do we seek and build relationships? We need to know ourselves, our mindset, and sense of efficacy as we build relationships with others. For students, learning from a trusted instructor usually results in having more freedom to make mistakes and learn from them. Before any of us can create those relationships with students, we must be comfortable with our own learning and being known by those with whom we work. Relationships and trust are developed in part by doing what we say we are going to do. This is a critical component of Data Team work—commitment and follow-through.

I Focus on Learning and the Language of Learning

Are you known as a learner? The more that we are known for our own learning, the more others around us will be drawn to learning. For many educators, the passion of helping others learn was a huge factor in choosing a vocation. Let's think about being more intentional about having more conversations about learning; it is the purpose for all our work.

We started this chapter by addressing that we need to intentionally build our own personal confidence. Along with this, we need to continually grow in our competence as educators. Our competence should lead us to choose to be more actively involved in our collaborative teams, in our individual classrooms, and in our schools and systems.

QUESTIONS TO CONSIDER

1. Why did I go into teaching? How has my passion changed? How could I allow my "why" to actually drive my work now?
2. During this past week, when did I feel as if I were having more of a fixed mindset? When did I feel as if I were having more of a growth mindset? What were these experiences like? How can I learn from them?
3. Of the ten mindframes, which are those that I am incorporating most into my practice now? Which do I want to incorporate more in my work going forward? How will I begin doing so?

2 How Do We Move from Compliant Committees to Effective Teams?

To go fast, go alone. To go far, go together.

—African proverb

Teamwork has always been important in the workplace; two or more heads are usually better than one when tackling problems, and education is no different from other fields in that respect. Throughout 2020, the COVID-19 pandemic shone a bright spotlight on teacher collaboration. Many teachers gained a new appreciation of each other as they left their schools and were forced to work from home. Others felt like they were left behind and isolated. Still others said that remote learning magnified what was going on in their daily practice.

What did this new era of distance learning expose about our practices as educators?

Some teams regularly met at the appointed times, filled out the appropriate forms, and decided how to remediate and intervene. Some teams did far less, only looking at data, not really changing instruction. Was the team you were part of stuck in a compliance rut?

At one elementary school where we have consulted, third-grade math fluency scores showed only 24 percent of students fluent in the spring of the year. A professional learning community (PLC) meeting was held with a month of school remaining. It at first seemed that those scores would be the final report for the year. As the team talked, the question was raised, "What if we actually intervened in order to improve those scores?" The dialogue then took off; there was so much energy in the room. The group decided to recruit every teacher in every school to help increase fluency. Strategies were suggested, and instructional practices were reviewed. For three weeks after the meeting, *everyone* mobilized. There was excitement that had not been present previously. After the three weeks, everyone wanted to see what the revised results could be. Eighty-two percent of students were now fluent! Teachers, instructional coaches, and students celebrated. Their pride pulsated throughout the building. There was a clear sense of "we did it" and "we did it together." The old adage that success breeds success became reality because this group of educators realized they could accomplish anything they set their minds to that spring—all to the great benefit of their students.

This is just one of many examples of collective efficacy that we have witnessed over the years. Short-term goals are met with focused team efforts.

This particular success story originated in Joliet, Illinois. Dr. Tricia Nagel of the district office gives this important summary of what happened.

INSIGHTS FROM COLLEAGUES

Dr. Tricia Nagel, director of curriculum and instruction, Joliet, Illinois

Using the Data Team process, a group of instructional coaches and teachers increased mathematical fluency skills. They measured growth of over 60 percent. They did this by adding additional instructional strategies to make math fun. The coaches dedicated themselves to concentrate on the fluency standards in the teacher PLCs. They used the coaching cycle, instituting a building-wide fluency event to promote their goals.

Dr. Nagel also notes that the scores were maintained to the next grade level in the fall. That is the second part of the story. After spring testing, as everyone celebrated, the question was raised, "How can we know the skills have been mastered?" Once again, the dialogue among team members took off. The instructional coaches mobilized again; they distributed manipulatives and interactive work for students to do during the summer. They added online games students could do. They used a robocall to let parents know about math fluency goals for the summer. Twice during the summer, the coaches and teachers sent mailings to the families to encourage them to get excited about math. In the first week of school the following year, the students were assessed again. The 82 percent proficiency rate held.

Angela was part of a middle school team that experienced a similar phenomenon in which the improvements made in the spring held in the fall. This eighth-grade team in South Carolina had worked hard for several months, having their students write expository and persuasive essays every two weeks (alternating the types). These essays were collaboratively scored using an abbreviated rubric derived from the rubric used on the state test. In every two-week cycle following essay writing, the team (representing all content areas) addressed weaknesses by implementing several innovative instructional strategies, including a graphic organizer combined with a slogan and gestures. On the last assessment before state testing occurred in the spring, 80 percent of the eighth graders were proficient. The seventh-grade team had also adopted a similar process (because of the eighth-grade team's success) and had about 75 percent of their students scoring proficient in the spring as well. When the seventh graders were promoted to eighth grade in the fall, the outgoing eighth-grade team gave a baseline writing prompt to check to see how well the students could perform. About 75 percent of students scored proficient on this first writing prompt. The team was so excited to pick up from that point forward, not having to remediate things they had had to remediate in past years. They could immediately add rigor and depth and keep supporting these student writers who were well on their way to becoming excellent.

A favorite quotation about collective teacher efficacy comes from an article in *Educational Leadership*, "When teams of educators believe they have the ability to make a difference, exciting things can happen in a school" (Donohoo, Hattie, and Eells, 2018, p. 40). This is what happened in the math third-grade team in Illinois and the eighth-grade team in South Carolina. Teachers believed they could—and they did.

For purposes of this chapter, it is important to be clear about what collective teacher efficacy is, how to build an effective and safe team, how to design team groupings that work for each building, and what to expect as teams learn to work together.

What Is Collective Teacher Efficacy?

Albert Bandura's name appears in all education psychology courses. Bandura was fascinated by people and what gave them confidence. He first coined the term *collective efficacy* in the 1970s; since that time the research and studies have continued. Jenni Donohoo (2017) in her book *Collective*

Efficacy builds on Bandura's theory. Let's discuss self-efficacy, collective efficacy, and collective teacher efficacy.

- Self-efficacy is an individual's belief that he or she can perform the necessary activities to attain a desired outcome. It is about both competence and confidence (and was addressed in Chapter 1).
- Collective efficacy is the belief that a group can achieve what they set out to do together. Collective efficacy is what school faculties count on to reach student achievement goals.
- Collective teacher efficacy (CTE) goes one step further and refers to teachers knowing that together, they can teach students effectively and help them learn more than ever.

Many educators talk about CTE but may not fully understand it or its implications. Some educators aren't sure why we need to know what seems like another buzzword, so we need to clarify its importance.

John Hattie's (2012) research is key here. His work examines positive and negative effects on student achievement and is based on a synthesis of more than 1,500 meta-analyses. The scope of his research includes over 80 million students. It is perhaps the largest scale and most influential research ever conducted in education.

According to Hattie, a .40 effect size is the value where a student would gain a year's growth for a year's time invested. Strategies and programs that achieve an effect size higher than .40 would then be considered highly effective. Collective teacher efficacy has a 1.57 effect size on student achievement. This is the most powerful influence on student learning in all of John Hattie's work. This is clearly one of the strongest "whys" for working as a Data Team. The path to continuous school improvement and increased student learning must incorporate effective teams who are actively involved in building collective teacher efficacy.

The next step tackles just how efficacious teams are built.

How Do We Build Efficacious Teams?

The combination of tracking the evidence and collaborating about high-yield strategies is key to school improvement. Kimberly Miles gives us one evaluation.

INSIGHTS FROM COLLEAGUES

Dr. Kimberly Miles, East Gresham Elementary, Oregon

Our school turnaround efforts at East Gresham Elementary School had at their core collaborative work. The foundation included developing teacher teams and their collective efficacy for shared decision making based on analysis of data to identify strengths and challenges of the current practice. Professional learning and growth we did in collective efficacy and instructional improvement continue to inspire our teaching and learning systems in order to support more equitable outcomes for each of our students.

Most PLC teams that we have supported are able to design the "what" of collaborative work. The "how" of examining data and reflecting on it to change instructional practices is generally more unfamiliar. Some groups identify what work to do, and even *why* it is important. However, they leapfrog right over the process of group formation and can neither demonstrate the key attributes of collective teacher efficacy nor functionally implement "fresh" instruction customized for the needs of their students.

In practical terms, it becomes clear that consultants, districts, schools, and even teachers themselves move too quickly from the why to "just tell me what I need to do and I'll do it," because they are pressured to address their school and system mandates. Compliance becomes the default system. By being merely compliant, they leave behind the true power of small, collaborative groups who could change the school. They also leave behind the students in their classrooms, never achieving the stellar results they could. Consider this description from Principal Kim Gordon.

INSIGHT FROM COLLEAGUES

Kim Gordon, elementary principal, Joliet, Illinois

Collective teacher efficacy is one of those messy, iterative, relational processes that drive us linear, left-brained, analytic types crazy. We know we need it, though, because our beloved data tells us that high levels of CTE will result in the best outcomes for kids. The data also tells us that CTE is completely within our locus of control—it does not depend on the students, their families, the community, or any of the hundreds of other factors influencing achievement. Therefore, raising the level of CTE is achievable, and when we do, we will drive learning to new heights, *quod erat demonstrandum*.

So where to begin? We know that mastery experiences, vicarious experiences, social persuasion, and affective states are the four sources of CTE, and Data Teams are certainly a place where these four processes can flourish. However, I posit that to fulfill the promise of CTE, we must concurrently pursue and cultivate trust. Trust is the oil in the machine. Trust will increase the efficiency (and efficacy!) of the four sources and ensure that they support and improve CTE.

One strategy that builds trust, provides vicarious experience, enhances affective states, and can lead to mastery experiences is peer observation. Peer observation also increases teachers' knowledge of each other's work, which is one of the key enabling conditions for high CTE. Seeing is believing. When teachers observe each other, they gain valuable insight, they see new practices in action, their relationships and respect for each other improve, and trust is strengthened. As a result, they are more open to new ideas and collaborate more effectively during Data Teams conversations. I advise school leaders to advocate and provide resources for peer observation in conjunction with Data Teams to develop optimal conditions to reap the rewards of high collective teacher efficacy.

The trust that Kim describes doesn't just happen. This is one of the central components of the work that is sometimes assumed because we are all educators. Assuming that trust exists may be efficient, but not often very effective.

It is to be expected with Data Teams that there will be challenges at first. Fisher, Frey, and Smith (2020) in *The Teacher Credibility and Collective Efficacy Playbook* remind readers, "Initial efforts [in collective efficacy] will likely include struggle and failures. How teams respond to those struggles will either build or tarnish their collective efficacy. Over time, as teams become more efficacious, they will establish more challenging goals for themselves and their students, and learning will accelerate" (p. 248). This is once again, the intersection of self-efficacy and collective efficacy.

What individuals do and think at the personal level becomes what they contribute to the team and school. Do we as educators believe that we are more collaborative in our data-driven work today than we were five or six years ago? When this question was put to Principal James Bozeman, this is what he had to say.

INSIGHTS FROM COLLEAGUES

James Bozeman, assistant principal, LaGrange High School, LaGrange, Georgia

Asking someone to do something to produce a desired outcome, yet not equipping them with the means by which to do it, may not yield that desired result. Regardless of how many groups you form, graphs you create, or meetings you hold, gathering and using data can create either a positive or negative culture. On some level I think we, at LaGrange High School, have always focused on being data driven. However, producing data that is useful on all levels to advance direct goals can be challenging.

To produce a true data-driven culture at LHS, leadership had to be intentional in our approach. Teachers have participated in professional learning (PL) to the point that our mindset regarding it had become mundane. That had to be changed. Once we determined our school's focus, that is, allowing data to drive decision-making practices regardless of area, we knew we had to provide PL that would intentionally equip teachers with the means to accomplish it. Changing the mindset of staff can be challenging; if done correctly, it can foster practices that can change instruction and student achievement.

Instead of creating PL that teachers would brush off, we challenged them with mindset training that required them to do some self-reflection. If we were going to approach the gathering and use of data, or simply the term *data*, with a fixed mindset, we were going to continue producing the same results, never advancing. Once we had teachers' attention, data collection became more purposeful. We equipped our teachers with ideas and practices that allowed them to gather, break down, and use data information to reach the desired instructional goal.

Some teams find themselves sitting in meetings that need to happen, but individuals don't believe that they have freedom to speak, or fear that they won't be heard, or just plain want to get to their own work for today's class. The next section examines how teams become effective in their interactions.

The Stages in Forming Teams Safely

Dr. Timothy Clark (2020) describes four stages of psychological safety that represent a continuum of what a group must experience to become effective. As teachers become an effective team, they learn how to bring that same safety and encouragement to their own classrooms. At the same time, they bring the strength of their collaborative decisions, informed by student learning and achievement and designed by their teams. Imagine the possibilities of school transformation. Let's examine the process described by Clark.

"Psychological safety is a condition in which one feels included, safe to learn, safe to contribute, and safe to challenge the status quo—all without fear of being embarrassed, marginalized, or punished in some way" (p. 2). In Data Team work, this becomes central if the team is to move from being compliant to becoming effective.

The four stages a team must move through are

1. Inclusion safety
2. Learner safety
3. Contributor safety
4. Challenger safety

Inclusion safety is all about being included on the team. This goes beyond simply who has been assigned to the group by the administration. Do all members of the team actually feel welcome? For Data Team work, this means that all members of the team are accepted by all members of the team. This takes intentional building of communication between group members and collegiality beyond playing nice during meetings. Administration, team leaders, and team members must all work to ensure this acceptance is created and sustained.

Learner safety centers on each member having a voice. Are all members encouraged to ask questions or float an idea without eye-rolling by other members? Each educator feels safe in sharing of ideas, mistakes, credit for success, and certainly celebrations. The team must intentionally seek input and feedback from each member. It is important for both the team leader and team members to continuously monitor learner safety.

Contributor safety occurs when all voices are actually heard. This requires trust among the team members. Do members understand boundaries and keep the mutually established norms? With contributor safety, each member grows in their own competence and confidence, which allows for more effective practices that increase student learning.

Challenger safety allows members to push back on the status quo or the current evidence without ridicule or hostility. Can team members be candid with each other, disagree with each other, and still work together in the meeting? To design effective instructional practices for students, it is essential that we have a diversity of perspectives.

Intentional awareness of these four stages is important. Implementing and intentionally practicing these stages can transform educators as individuals and thus transform the work. Ideally, teachers are then able to take these practices to their classrooms and beyond. As we grow in our understanding of the four stages, we begin to enhance both our collaboration and the impact it can have on us.

Effective collaboration changes culture and clearly can move us away from mere compliance. When a team practices inclusion, encourages learning, provides opportunities to contribute, and ensures it is safe for members to challenge doing things as they've always been done, everyone benefits. Firestone, Cruz, and Rodl (2020) researched the power of teacher groups studying together and said, "Compared to other models of professional development, teacher study groups have a positive impact on teachers' knowledge and daily practice—and on student learning" (p. 675). Why? Because they have:

- Specific focus
- Active learning
- Coherence
- Duration
- Collective participation
- Expert input
- Tight connection to day-to-day practice

This is what Data Teams can be. Every one of the above attributes are built into the Clark model and all of collective efficacy. That leads us right to the next step in the process: forming teams.

The Formation of Teams

Data Teams can be organized in a number of ways but are joined together through the use of a common formative assessment or by data that is collected in common (such as data on reading levels or the number of credits earned toward graduation). There is no "right" size for a Data Team. Some of them consist of only two people, and others are as large as a dozen people. It is important to remember that it's not the size of the team that matters—it's the work that matters. The team is bound together in its duty to support all the students represented on the team. Collective efficacy cannot be achieved without the team members deeply invested in the success of all students represented by the team members.

There are four types of Data Teams that may be formed: horizontal, vertical, special needs or focus, and singleton. Let's start with horizontal teams.

Horizontal Teams

A horizontal Data Team is one that covers an entire grade level. So, in an elementary school, a second-grade team would consist of all second-grade teachers in the school. Others may be part of this team as well. For example, if there is a special education teacher who serves many of the second-grade students, they would be a natural fit for the team (see Figure 2.1). And, in elementary schools, physical education, music, and art teachers often serve as part of a specific grade-level team; these members are often able to add richness to the team's dialogue because of the different ways in which they interact with students.

At the middle school level, a horizontal team would consist of teachers of various subjects. For example, a seventh-grade team would consist of the teachers of the four core academic areas (English language arts, mathematics, science, social studies) at minimum (Figure 2.2). Angela was part of a middle school team that consisted of two ELA teachers, two math teachers, two science teachers, two social studies teachers, a special education teacher, and a physical education teacher. This team was large, with ten members. On an interdisciplinary team such as this one, the team

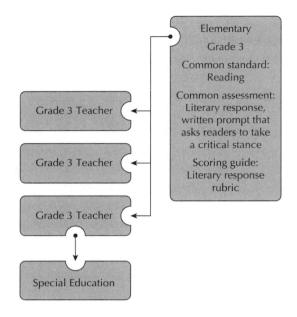

FIGURE 2.1   Example of a Horizontal Data Team

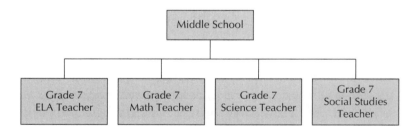

FIGURE 2.2   Horizontal Team, Middle School

must determine an area of focus that impacts all subject areas, like writing answers to text-dependent questions or drawing conclusions after reading, and create assessment tasks accordingly.

In some cases, a horizontal team may consist of small clusters of subject areas. For example, my own Data Team could have been configured with the science and math teachers as one team (four members) and the English language arts and social studies teachers as another (four members). The special education teacher could have been added to one group of four, and the PE teacher to the other, resulting in two teams of five members in this scenario.

Another possibility would be to have pairs as teams—two ELA teachers, two math teachers, two science teachers, and two social studies teachers.

At the high school level, horizontal teams are rare, but are sometimes used in academy-type settings or for specialized needs. So an eleventh-grade team of teachers who work with students in a criminal justice major may be grouped together as a Data Team even though they teach courses ranging from American literature to forensic science. Likewise, a ninth-grade team may work together to ease the transition from middle school to high school for students and may include teachers of academics in addition to electives like physical education and computer technology. (However, the most common configuration of Data Teams at the high school level is by the specific course being taught, not across courses.)

With the makeup of horizontal teams understood, let's review vertical teams.

Vertical Teams

A vertical team is so named because it includes teachers from multiple grade levels. A common configuration of this kind of team occurs at the middle or high school level as a department team. So a middle school English language arts Data Team might include all the teachers of that subject in sixth, seventh, and eighth grades (Figure 2.3). This type of team would

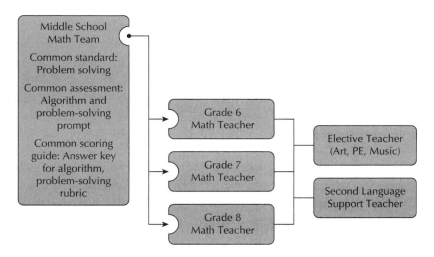

FIGURE 2.3   Example of a Vertical Data Team

select an identified student learning need that impacts each grade level, such as making valid inferences when reading or acquiring necessary academic vocabulary for further study in the discipline. Again, the need drives the creation of the assessment that the team uses.

An example of a high school vertical team could be all teachers who teach Algebra 1, across the grade levels. This type of team could first zero in on any needs the students demonstrate with the prerequisite skills for success in the course. Later, the team would focus on the critical concepts and skills necessary in this foundational math course. Ideally, students at all grade levels who are enrolled in Algebra 1 would achieve success by the end of the year.

Another example of a high school vertical team would be a team of ninth- and tenth-grade English teachers. Because many state English language arts standards are now written in grade spans of two years (9–10 and 11–12), these teams representing two grade levels have become more common. In our experience, these teams often choose to focus on argumentative writing for their formative assessments.

Elementary schools can have vertical teams, too, especially if they are departmentalized at the upper grade levels. So, for example, several teachers of English language arts at fourth and fifth grades could be one team, and several teachers of math at fourth and fifth grades would comprise another team. In small schools where there is just one main teacher per grade level, we have seen a kindergarten and first-grade team of two teachers, a second- and third-grade team of two teachers, and a fourth- and fifth-grade team of two teachers. In some of these schools, the students also "loop" for two years of instruction, so the team of teachers and the entire group of students remain the same for the entire loop. These teams often work on skills that appear in the standards for multiple grade levels and that are cross-curricular in nature, like citing evidence and problem-solving.

Special needs or focus teams are the third type of Data Team that can be formed.

Special Needs or Focus Teams

A special needs or focus team is formed based on a specific area of need that students have demonstrated. For example, the freshman year of high school is often a difficult transition time for students, so a ninth-grade transition team that consists of various adults who interact with those students could be formed. In this case, the team's data may come from periodic surveys of students and from information on attendance, tardiness, discipline, and course grades. The team could include the Grade 9 English and math teachers, the counselor and administrator who work most closely with ninth-grade students, and other professionals who may be important to the students' success, like the school social worker (Figure 2.4).

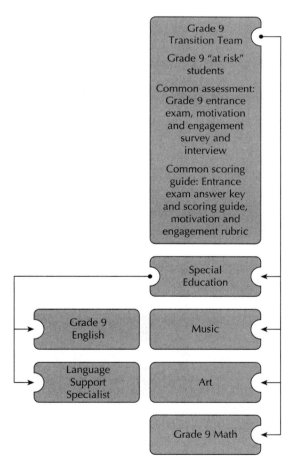

FIGURE 2.4   Example of a Specialist Data Team

Another type of specialist team at the high school level might be for seniors, focusing on college and career readiness. This team would be configured similarly to the ninth-grade team just discussed, but might carefully monitor data about course credits earned and college and internship applications submitted in addition to data from common formative assessments.

At the middle school level, a special needs or focus team might be formed to concentrate on eighth-grade students who are overage or otherwise at risk of failing. This team would closely monitor multiple sources of data on these students and take action in response so that the largest number of students possible would enter high school prepared for success.

At the elementary level, a special needs or focus team might be created to monitor the progress of all children who are reading at least one grade level below the current grade. This team could include representative teachers from each grade, the literacy coach, the school media specialist, and others who would enact strategies to support these students—strategies that complement what the grade-level Data Teams and school administrators do to move those same students ahead in their reading.

Finally, let's consider singleton teams, the fourth type of Data Team that may be formed.

Singleton Teams

In many large middle and high schools, there are teachers who teach courses that no other teachers in the building teach—known as singletons. Subjects often include family and consumer sciences, business technology, ROTC, world languages, health sciences, building trades, criminal justice, and auto technology. Often, principals place the teachers of these widely disparate courses on a team together and direct them to meet when other Data Teams are meeting. However, these teams often struggle to find meaningful data to discuss and respond to. We recommend that these teams find a common focus that they agree to work on in their classes—for example, reading complex text in the discipline or learning domain-specific terminology—and bring student work samples to meetings to examine.

Whether your Data Team is structured as a vertical, horizontal, special needs or focus, or singleton team, it will become successful only if everyone on the team works together.

Working Together as a Team

Bruce Tuckman (1965), a psychologist, first proposed his model of group development in the 1960s, and it remains pertinent. His model includes stages called forming, storming, norming, and performing. He postulates that all these stages are necessary and must occur for any team to deliver results. While moving through these stages is necessary, the progress is often frustrating for both team members and administrators alike. However, understanding the stages can be beneficial for anyone involved with the work of Data Teams, just as understanding Piagetian psychology or Bloom's Taxonomy of Educational Objectives is helpful when teaching students. Along with Clark's stages of psychological safety discussed earlier, Tuckman's work can help teams move from compliance to true collective efficacy.

Briefly, the forming stage of team development involves individuals trying to get along and avoid conflict. This stage often manifests itself as newly formed Data Teams busy themselves with organizational and logistical tasks, such as deciding where and when to meet and figuring out how to keep records like meeting minutes and data displays. Team members also spend time getting better acquainted with each other on a personal level. This stage is characterized by little work of significance; it is basically a "getting to know you" time.

Data Team leaders, instructional coaches, and administrators often grow impatient during this forming phase because they want each team to focus immediately on the student learning needs. However, a team cannot effectively address student learning needs until they have experienced the forming phase and have started creating psychological safety. Like an algebra problem, the mix of friendships, personalities, and experience on each team creates a different formula for the length of the forming stage. Some teams move through it in a meeting or two; other teams can take much longer.

The next stage is called storming. In this stage, team members turn their attention to the problems that must be solved—for Data Teams, that means the student learning challenges that must be addressed. Tuckman's theory posits that some groups move through this stage very quickly, while others never leave it. Data Team leaders, instructional coaches, and administrators from both the building and system level often try to intervene if this stage appears to last too long. Sometimes these efforts work with the existing team members, but in other cases the configuration of the team has to be changed. A change in team membership is an extreme solution but is one that is sometimes cautiously exercised by administrators.

Storming includes team members presenting their own views, which sometimes lead to controversy or conflict because they may differ drastically from the views of teammates. On some Data Teams, teachers may express ideas about student learning capabilities that are offensive to other members, such as, "Those particular kids will never be able to learn this. They just don't have what it takes. Why don't we just move on?" Another common problem during the storming stage is when one or two members share their instructional strategy ideas and don't entertain the suggestions of others; for example, "Here's the way to teach that. I've taught it that way for years and it's the only way the kids get it. I don't see why we're wasting time trying to come up with other methods." These kinds of statements prolong the storming stage because they don't encourage dialogue and don't enhance psychological safety.

Those in supervisory, coaching, or team leadership positions can help teams move through the storming phase by guiding the dialogue. They can model effective ways to present ideas and can take statements such as the ones given previously and paraphrase them so that they become less definitive and more inviting. Many Data Team leaders grow frustrated during the storming phase, as they feel ill-equipped to handle the strong emotions that may be displayed by their colleagues. Data Team leaders who do grow frustrated need additional support from administrators or outside experts. Some Data Teams actually study information about group development prior to beginning the meeting cycle so that they are prepared for what's ahead.

The next stage in team development is norming. In this often long-awaited stage, the team manages to have a shared goal and a consensual plan for reaching it. Team members have learned that sometimes they have to forego their own ideas, or at the very least find ways to combine their ideas with the ideas of others. In this stage, agreement is reached fairly easily, whereas in earlier stages, it was not. In the norming stage, members have all taken responsibility and are keeping their commitments. They are all working toward the common good. From this point forward, a Data Team can be highly effective.

The last stage teams reach is the stage called performing. High-performing teams function interdependently and are able to do what's required with ease. Team members are motivated to do the work of the group, and direct supervision or guidance from outside members (like administrators) is not necessary. These are the teams that meet even when they don't have to. They enjoy and learn from their collaboration and feel that their teaching would not be as effective without it. The performing stage is the desired state for all Data Teams, because it is in this state that students can benefit the most.

Each team needs to take time to think deeply about its work. If the goal is to be efficient, there is often compliance involved. Compliance is about doing the job. Collaboration is about coming together to do the work. Timothy Clark encourages us to take care to internally build teams that keep our work authentic. Bruce Tuckman extends our thinking, giving us the process steps of team-building to be effective. Intentional implementation of both makes all the difference!

QUESTIONS TO CONSIDER

1. What three words would I use to describe my experience with PLCs or Data Teams thus far?
2. When have I experienced each of the four stages of psychological safety? (This may be an example from outside education.)
3. Have I been part of a high-performing team? If so, how did we move through the stages of team development? Can I apply anything to my current teamwork?
4. What could I change to positively affect the teams on which I am currently serving?

3 Collecting Evidence and Using It Effectively

Data Teams are the single best way to help educators . . . move from "drowning in data" to using information to make better instructional decisions.

—Doug Reeves and Tony Flach, "Meaningful Analysis Can Rescue Schools from Drowning in Data"

Some educators have grown tired of terms like *data-driven* and *evidence-based*. However, the process that an effective Data Team follows is rooted in data—and by data, we mean information about how and what students are learning.

Bringing up the concept of data sometimes interrupts productive teacher conversations about learning. Perhaps it is because teachers tend to become passive recipients of data interpretation rather than seeing it as a way to celebrate success or even as a flare signaling that it's time to change direction. Some teachers have also been victims of data being wielded like a hammer rather than a spark leading to positive next steps in the classroom and in the building. Dr. Adam Drummond writes in *The Instructional Change Agent* (2019) that "frequently tracking student data provides the opportunities to discuss specific high-yield strategies needed to increase performance" (p. 104). The key is that evidence is seen as valuable because it is used so regularly. As Dr. Drummond discusses, leadership at this point is central to success. Is the regular collection of data happening and is it part of conversations around student learning? Let's explore that question.

Collecting Evidence

One team in Minnetonka, Minnesota, found themselves needing to make major changes when the COVID-19 pandemic hit. The school went to

100 percent virtual learning. Brent Veninga and Lisa Patrick share their feedback from students that provided important evidence for their PLC work during virtual instruction.

INSIGHTS FROM COLLEAGUES

Brent Veninga and Lisa Patrick, Minnetonka, Minnesota

While every district and classroom is as unique as the students they serve, virtual education in a co-teaching environment presented both unique opportunities and significant challenges. Our experience was unique in that our course is team taught; we combine both Global Studies and Advanced Placement Environmental Science. Even though our courses are unique, the big ideas overlap and prove essential to our student outcomes. Our PLC received this feedback from one student, when asked what advice would help future students: "Understand the large overlying themes and the rest is fairly simple." This told us we needed to frontload more about where we were going with our learning goals.

Initial PLC work consisted of planning implementation and delivery of new technology tools, shifting educational priorities, and incorporation of new synchronous and asynchronous learning models in a distance e-learning environment. By the end of the semester, multiple virtual rooms and tools were incorporated into the students' work.

During this early triage stage, priorities shifted to focus on both the needs of our students in a virtual environment and on our families in the smaller spaces of their homes. Simply scheduling PLC time for both instructors to meet was a challenge. Our model incorporates project-based and experiential learning; we revised deliverables for the students based on our PLC conversations.

In our new model of educational delivery, students shared the need for increased time on their AP course. In our PLC, we shifted to focus on that priority. We changed both the structure of the day and the instructional practices. We gathered important feedback from student surveys. Here are a few items:

- "I liked the fact that we met almost every single class period. Spending too much time away from teachers kind of would feel like wasted time, but these teachers used their time well and tried to keep us engaged."
- "The whole-class and small-group conferences worked well. The small groups especially gave students the ability to collaborate and create with others."

(Continued)

- "Every morning he posts on his updates a rundown of our day. He then begins every morning with a conference, explaining our day and beginning the first activity."

Throughout the quarter, a number of critical themes emerged:

- Experiencing and giving everyone (including ourselves!) grace and leeway as we face enormous challenges
- A greater emphasis on the role of the PLC
- Rhythm, routine, and daily flow
- Determining whether the content/purpose is better in an asynchronous or synchronous environment; aim for a balance
- Truly differentiated instruction
- Evidence-based decision making
- Modeling adaptability and resilience
- Finding ways to share the collective workload
- Back channel communications proved a necessity

Brent and Lisa effectively incorporated the evidence from students to identify their next steps. They were truly reflective practitioners who were looking at their practice (as much as possible) from students' eyes.

The word *evidence* means more than numbers on a page or a spreadsheet. It is larger than a score on an assessment. Evidence must be the focus of a Data Team's work. Quantitative data is the statistical snapshot of the collected evidence. Qualitative data is broader and includes the context surrounding the statistics, feedback that students offer, and much more. Perhaps a nonthreatening and accurate synonym for *data* is *information*—and, in the context of Data Teams, it is information that focuses squarely on student learning.

To understand what and how students are learning, educators must collect both quantitative and qualitative evidence. Robert Culp looks at the two types of data.

INSIGHTS FROM COLLEAGUES

Dr. Robert Culp, instructional coach, Joliet, Illinois

Educators need to confront the questions "What constitutes data?" and "Will the data truly assist in driving instruction?" When asked to collect data, we often fall into the trap of valuing quantitative data, such as a test that can be easily scored and given a percentage, over qualitative data such as conferring with students or anecdotal notes. It is important when examining data to ensure that we are not valuing one form over another; specifically, valuing quantitative data over qualitative data. When this occurs, we take the human components away from the data. That's not to say quantitative data is not valuable.

There is a tension between quantitative and qualitative inquiry models; often with proponents feeling that one is better than the other. "Proponents of the two approaches often treat them as contrasting ideologies, tenaciously and, occasionally, dogmatically held" and often push for others "to embrace the creed of the 'one right way'" (Schwandt, 1989, p. 379). The truth is both have their value and when they work together, give us a whole picture. For Data Team meetings to have focus, we need to ensure we are truly examining our students as a whole entity, as humans, and not just as a sole data point. When we do this, our data-driven instruction keeps the focus on the student and not just a single data point. Have we selected learning progressions intentionally? Are we collecting the evidence that clearly indicates that they are learning? If students aren't, what can we do about it? If they are, how do we celebrate and keep going?

The central key here is to collect evidence in multiple ways. Doug Fisher, Nancy Frey, John Almarode, Karen Flories, and David Nagel (2020) suggest in *The PLC+ Playbook* that these four general types of information be collected:

- Analysis of recent student work samples;
- Short interviews with a representative sample of students;
- Recent initial and end-of-unit assessment results; and
- Student feedback about a recently completed unit study.

Data Teams that are highly effective regularly assess students, but they also examine other data (like the four types above). They are also astute observers of (and reflectors on) their teaching. Their skills in seeing their own teaching from another perspective—and acting on what they learn from that examination—allow them to continually become more responsive teachers.

Data collection is imperative; it must be used effectively to have value.

Using Evidence Effectively

Establishing a culture that is comfortable with data and uses it along with other evidence to frame its work is critical in order to be a true professional learning community. In a series of three Insights from Colleagues, you will find a close look from multiple perspectives on data and its importance within a school. We begin with the principal of LaGrange High School.

INSIGHT FROM COLLEAGUES

Alton White, principal, LaGrange High School, LaGrange, Georgia

Every organization produces data to inform stakeholders, monitor performance, and determine areas to focus on for improvement. Corporations publish earnings reports and projections. Athletic teams keep track of more data than the average fan could possibly use. It makes no sense that education would be any different. We have to be willing to be transparent and share our data with stakeholders, and then we have to be willing to use that data in making decisions. This creates a data-driven culture that will lead to true systemic school improvement that will last over time.

The first step is getting teachers to be willing to own the data. It is what it is. Data does not lie. And in a school, it is important to know that it is our data as a school, not just any teacher's individual data. Just because a teacher may teach U.S. History to juniors doesn't mean that that the U.S. History test scores belong to just that teacher. Those teachers who taught them in ninth and tenth grade own that data, too. Reading comprehension, writing, and critical thinking skills all play a part in those test scores. As school leaders, we have to have conversations assuring teachers that first the data belongs to everyone, and probably more importantly that data will not be used as a "gotcha" tool. Then, it is critical to live by this. Teachers must be shown repeatedly over time that we are going to discuss data continuously for school improvement; it is not going to be used to negatively impact their evaluations. Failure to work to improve instruction, assessments techniques, etc., will impact their evaluations, but data by itself will not.

The most effective way to model this is to discuss and use data continuously. In every faculty meeting, and especially leadership team meetings, we look at some type of data. Test data, attendance data, failure rates, discipline, etc. Teachers begin to realize we are going to use data in making decisions at the school level; they begin to see the importance of using it in their departments and classrooms. Once this becomes the norm at the school level, you can begin to make it the norm for teachers as well.

You have to let teachers know what expectations you have of them as far as disaggregating data and how to use it. We make them participate in common planning with others in their department who teach the same or similar subjects. We conducted professional learning sessions on what data to look at, how to pull that data, and how to collaborate. Administrators worked with teachers initially to make sure everyone was comfortable with the process. Then we held them accountable by attending collaborative planning sessions and/or having them report to us what they were doing.

The most effective practice has been to have teacher leaders, who feel comfortable with the process and can show the positive impact it has had on their students, lead professional learning sessions. During this time there are no administrators present. This has led to ownership by the teachers; once they bought in and took ownership, it became the norm. Now teachers request data from us. Recently, my special ed department head asked me to run discipline data for special ed students. New scheduling models were implemented to try to address some behaviors that were causing students to miss instructional time. She wanted to see if the new model was effective. She told me, "I feel like it's been better, but I need to look at the data to see if there has really been a difference." These types of requests have become more of the norm now. When teachers begin to see positive results for themselves or their colleagues—the process sells itself!

How did success happen at LaGrange? As in Joliet, Illinois, once teachers see that the evidence is useful, then there is no stopping a team. Math teacher Lindsey Trinrud gives a terrific overview of how the data-driven culture grew.

INSIGHTS FROM COLLEAGUES

Lindsey Trinrud, math teacher, LaGrange High School, LaGrange, Georgia

In the past five years I have seen my school develop a strong data-driven culture. Principal Alton White has helped teachers develop ways to collect, analyze, and understand data. He developed a team of teacher leaders who worked with their peers to grow a culture of collaboration. Teachers began to look at data through a team perspective instead of a "which teacher is best" perspective. Data became a way to identify areas of improvement, practices that were effective or ineffective, and develop research-based professional learning that was relevant to *our* school, staff, and students. By collaborating in common courses, departments, and across the entire school, teachers began to use data not as a grade but as a tool to create a better learning experience for all students. Here's what we did at LHS:

- Collaboration was insisted upon. Teachers had to learn to work with each other. Departments built trust and communication. The staff as a whole began to have common conversations instead of being isolated into separate subject areas.
- Teachers collected and looked at data. In the beginning, this was just looking at numbers. It was a "who did better" activity. Once the collaboration culture began to shift, data became less personal.
- We started to look at data with more detail. This included subgroups and closer item analysis. We began to make connections with the data and what was happening in the classroom. Teachers began to connect what we saw in the data to practices in the classroom.
- When the teacher leadership team was developed, we spent more time on how to make looking at the data easier and more consistent for the whole staff. We developed common tools and professional learning to do this. This opened the door for further collaboration and conversations. As collaboration increased, the culture of the school became richer.
- Common courses, departments, and the staff as a whole began discussing trends in the data. We focused on things we saw and how we could address the needs of our students and staff. From here the teacher leadership team developed further professional learning to continue to help the staff develop best practices that were data-driven and research-based to create deeper learning for our students

Further reflecting on the data culture established at LaGrange from a teacher's perspective is Randy Hardigree.

INSIGHTS FROM COLLEAGUES

Randy Hardigree, biology teacher, LaGrange High School, LaGrange, Georgia

Most profoundly, I think Mr. White made data a catalyst for action instead of just numbers showing a "state of the school." For him personally, numbers drive creativity in finding ways to make a shift happen.

The idea of data is nothing new—it's what you do with it that is different. The graduation rate was nothing new, but prior to Mr. White's leadership, I don't think anybody had a frame of reference for what to do with it or about it. Creating unconventional pathways to a diploma was something I had never heard of before.

The failure rate was generally thought of as proof that we teach a broken demographic (kids who just aren't capable). To Mr. White, a high failure rate is an indicator that something must change about the way teaching and learning take place in the classroom. I realized that finding alternate ways to help students master content is not the same thing as lowering the bar.

In LHS Biology, we've been using aggregate data and focused item analysis to drive our instruction and remediation for many years. Data and evidence have affected the bigger picture: the whole school, the big picture of what we're doing as teachers. That's what I see from my perspective.

Our culture now shows a belief that students are our greatest asset, where it had historically been approached as if students were lucky to be in our school system jumping through our hoops.

As Randy shared about the biology teachers, evidence needs to be collected closest to the action to be effective. That is when teachers have more impact on real change and success in student learning. Any successful team needs to collectively identify and understand:

- Their standard as a whole;
- Learning targets or objectives derived from that standard;
- The learning progressions to achieve each learning target or objective; and
- The evidence that clearly shows that students have mastered the entire learning progression.

The evidence must consist of data, both quantitative and qualitative, that makes clear that learning is happening. So, what snafus keep the data from being used effectively? There are three possible pitfalls: a teacher's loss of faith that evidence makes a difference, causation error when interpreting the data, and design flaws in the assessment (usually a mismatch between the evidence elicited and the evidence required to show mastery of the learning targets). Let's first examine how to navigate a loss of faith.

Loss of Faith

In today's fast-paced, stress-producing schools, there is little time for teachers to breathe, let alone reflect on their desire to help students. Newer constraints, including those that surfaced during the COVID-19 pandemic, raise important questions, namely, "What do I want students to learn deeply?" and "How will I know from a distance or with limited contact time that they are truly learning?" Parker Palmer (1983), known for his rich insights in teaching and learning, reminds us, "It's not about the learner in the classroom, but about the teacher" (p. 44). As lead learner in the classroom, a teacher's sense of efficacy becomes the very wind in the sails empowering students to develop confidence in their own ability to learn.

Loss of faith can be mitigated as we allow ourselves to be transparent with our team and practice the collective efficacy described in Chapter 2. Professional learning that inspires us and experiencing some success also help. Kathryn Girard describes that experience.

INSIGHTS FROM COLLEAGUES

Kathryn Girard, fifth-grade teacher, East Gresham Elementary School, Oregon

Whenever I attend a professional development or a team meeting, I am always anxious for one particular part: the collaboration piece. This is a magical time where the experience of true collaboration brings out the best parts of me as a teacher. Let me briefly explain what I mean by true collaboration: it is not the sharing of all the things that are going well in your classroom. Rather it is the open, honest, and raw conversations that allow you to open yourself up and examine your successes and failures. It is a time to be vulnerable and have others help strengthen and expand your knowledge with their own expertise and experience. After a moment of true collaboration, I walk away feeling empowered and with an eagerness to get back in front of my students to execute all that I have learned.

The empowerment described here is powerful. Recall from Chapter 1 the principles of learning, having passion for teaching, and being ready to celebrate student learning. Kathryn understands that her own learning becomes the driver of renewed passion and creativity to help her students learn. Then as they, in turn, pick up that passion and succeed, the class celebrates together. Does it get better than that?

Let's take a closer look at the next pitfall of using data: causation errors.

Causation Errors

When teachers examine data or evidence, they are often pressured for time. They may be rushing against the clock in the team meeting to get forms filled out. At times this leads them to identify the wrong causes for the effects that appear in the evidence.

Searching for root causes is key to understanding how to address student need effectively. If a cause is misinterpreted, the entire learning progression can be in jeopardy.

This confusion about root cause occurred with a Data Team in Oregon. Teachers thought the students were struggling in one place, but it was actually another. Matt Wallace shares the story of what happened when the correct need was identified in a fourth-grade PLC.

INSIGHTS FROM COLLEAGUES

Matt Wallace, teacher, East Gresham Elementary School, Gresham, Oregon

I always considered myself a pretty good educator. I designed standards-based assessments, used learning targets, created engaging and rigorous lessons, offered quick checks for understanding, etc. In the end, I rarely saw the growth I was hoping for. Once we began our Data Team work in earnest, I recognized holes in my students learning that I hadn't seen before. These holes were making it difficult, if not impossible, for them to access the learning.

(Continued)

Data Teams are nothing new; they've been around for a while. While we spent time grading papers and entering scores, we spent little time actually looking at the work itself. Once we drilled down deeper, doing the "dirty" work, we began to notice these very specific holes and gaps in student learning. For example, our fourth and fifth graders had a history of low reading comprehension scores. This wasn't from a lack of programs, desire, or effort on the part of the teachers, families, or students. This was such a big problem that we didn't know where to begin. Data Teams helped us narrow our focus and identify the root cause. Turns out they had several holes in their phonics skills. They struggled with blends, digraphs, and vowels teams. Once we worked on filling those holes, reading scores increased and we were able to switch our focus to comprehension skills. Without the laser focus that the data teamwork provided us, our students would have continued to struggle and fall further behind.

The pitfall of misidentified cause or effect can be mitigated by the team raising enough questions with each other and not settling for the first possible cause. Daniel Venables (2014) has created an "I Notice, I Wonder" protocol in *Data into Action*. We have adapted variations of the protocol with teams that support their collaboration and use data effectively. Here is one adaptation of that process used with teams:

1. Each team member is given an index card.
2. When shown some data they are asked to write their response to this question: What do you notice about the data set?
3. Without speaking to each other, the facilitator shuffles and redistributes the cards to other team members to be read aloud.
4. The cards are read one at a time until all have been read (without any discussion or comment).
5. Each member turns over the card that they are holding.
6. They write responses to this question: What do you wonder about the data?
7. The new responses are reshuffled, redistributed, and read aloud (again without comment).
8. The discussion of these questions follows: What did we see? What did we wonder? What do we think now?

This is the very reason we have team meetings—to collaborate so that we become better together. The process outlined above can help move us toward that goal.

The third pitfall of data analysis is design flaws in the assessment. Let's take a closer look at it.

Design Flaws in the Assessment

When a common formative assessment is due, sometimes the rush is on. Teachers want to ensure that assessments present the evidence we need to know students are mastering the sequence of learning targets that lie before them. Effective assessment as part of Data Team work is crucial. Dr. Robert Culp, an instructional coach in Joliet, Illinois, shares more about this.

INSIGHTS FROM COLLEAGUES

Dr. Robert Culp, instructional coach, Joliet, Illinois

One of the most beneficial tasks we do as a Data Team is designing assessments together and determining the criteria for success. Successful Data Teams collaborate and go through a five-stage process:

1. Decide what data we want to attain and design the task/assessment.
2. Create a rubric collaboratively, ensuring it stays focused on the data we are collecting.
3. Several, if not all, team members complete the task/assessment to have examples.
4. The team grades the examples together to ensure all approach gathering data through the same lens.
5. Revise as needed.

This process of practicing "dogfooding," that is, using your own product before giving it to students, ensures Data Team conversations are focused and significant. Once we started utilizing this practice, our Data Teams found that the rubrics and assignments were often not gathering the data we thought they were, or were not quite as clear, focused, and universal as we had thought.

Now that we have implemented this as our norm, our Data Team meetings are more productive, focused, and truly assist in improving student achievement.

The mismatch of assessment can be mitigated by the collaborative discussions and actions taken by the team. Unpacking or unwrapping the standards is a necessary initial step. This ensures that the team is clear about what is to be learned, how it is to be learned, and what constitutes evidence of the learning.

Collecting the best evidence is challenging. We have examined the need for evidence, our attitudes about data, and the value of expanding our evidence to include student feedback. We raise questions in our analysis to show we have found the root cause or area for reteaching struggling students; we then ensure we are mindful of the most common pitfalls that cause teams to struggle. When we collect good evidence and see students learn and succeed, we take time to celebrate that learning.

QUESTIONS TO CONSIDER

1. What is my personal definition of the word *data* as it applies to this work?
2. What are three words that describe my current attitudes about collecting data? How have these attitudes helped or hindered my work?
3. How would I describe my colleagues' attitudes about collecting data?
4. What steps could I take to support colleagues in expanding their views of data?
5. What steps could my team take to ensure we are avoiding the pitfalls discussed in this chapter?

4   What Do I Really Know About This Work?

The use of professional learning communities is the best, least expensive, most professionally rewarding way to improve schools . . . Such communities hold out immense, unprecedented hope for schools and the improvement of teaching.

—Mike Schmoker, "No Turning Back"

Educators don't enter the Data Team process in a vacuum; neither do they enter it without valuable expertise and experience. This chapter is intended to illuminate the connections among your expertise and experience and Data Team collaboration. Additionally, it seeks to highlight the interconnectedness of Data Team collaboration and sound assessment and instruction practices.

Data Teams create and administer common formative assessments (CFAs) based on learning targets that represent full mastery of prioritized standards. They meet frequently to examine student work, including the data from these assessments, so that they can innovate to improve instruction. The work of Data Teams exhibits the true qualities of professional learning communities (PLCs) and helps educators collectively address long-term student achievement goals. When Data Teams are implemented effectively in a school, they are the vehicle that moves the school from a teaching organization to a learning organization.

Let's start with the evolution of educational standards.

What You Know About Standards

Teachers trained in the 1970s and 1980s (like the authors of this book) focused on several things in their education courses and student teaching: behavioral objectives, classroom management, and designing instruction to fill up time. Every minute was accounted for, and scope and sequence documents dictated the dozens of granular, measurable objectives that were to be mastered and checked off lists. But as the cognitive science field advanced and as educators became more aware of how memory works, teachers started planning and carrying out their work a bit differently.

In the early 1990s, concurrent with the advances in cognitive science, states began to create educational standards. These differed from the long lists of objectives that had existed in the past. The New Standards Project, a national movement initiated in 1991, "envisioned a curriculum built around standards defined by what students ought to know, not by time spent in class" (Hoff, 2001). This ambitious movement did not result in all states crafting new standards that were of the desired rigor, but 22 states and six large school districts were part of the project and did create new standards and assessments aligned with them. Many of these assessments were more performance-based than in the past. Many states decreased their reliance on long, multiple-choice tests and added components like essay writing, writing portfolios, and open-ended mathematical problem-solving. This evolution of large-scale assessment had huge impacts on teachers as they incorporated activities and assessments aligned with new state tests into their teaching.

The next huge wave of standards redesign began in 2010 with the development of the Common Core State Standards, initiated by the National Governors Association Center for Best Practices (Common Core State Standards Initiative, 2020). These standards were designed to address the lack of college and career readiness that governors, state school superintendents, and university faculty perceived. Teachers across the country were involved in creating and evaluating the standards. All but four states eventually adopted the Common Core (ASCD, 2020) and changed their state assessments significantly. If you have been teaching since 2010, you likely experienced changes in curriculum and assessment driven by the move to Common Core. When state assessments change, school system leaders usually orchestrate new waves of curriculum development so that curriculum and assessment are better aligned.

In the years since 2010, in response to public outcry and teacher pushback against the Common Core, many states purport to no longer use the Common Core State Standards. However, the standards states do use are clearly derived from Common Core. In some states, the new standards are practically verbatim Common Core.

The move toward standards actually began long before the New Standards Project and the Common Core initiative, however. Esteemed educational researcher Ralph Tyler (1949) first wrote about four basic principles of delivering curriculum and evaluating the resulting learning. This has become known as the Tyler Rationale and is built upon these four principles, which should seem familiar to you:

1. Defining appropriate learning objectives.
2. Establishing useful learning experiences.
3. Organizing learning experiences to have a maximum cumulative effect.
4. Evaluating the curriculum and revising those aspects that did not prove to be effective.

So, no matter when you started teaching, and no matter what standards your state or system has in place at this time, your teaching life has certainly been affected by standards! Let's unpack what you know about standards and how these standards are a critical component of Data Team–powered PLCs.

There most likely exists a set of standards that applies to every course, content area, and grade level you teach. For many of these standards, there are high-stakes tests that exist (that your students must take). If there are not high-stakes tests for some of the courses or content areas you teach, this doesn't relieve you from assessing student mastery of standards and reporting on that mastery. You still have to provide both students and families with information about student progress in terms of grade reporting (whether that's standards-based or using the traditional percentage method). Grades are just one form of feedback. The feedback that you give to students day in and day out is what moves them ever closer to mastery.

Standards are broad, comprehensive statements of what students must learn; they are not curriculum. In most cases, they do not delineate all the learning goals or targets that students must meet to have mastered them fully. This is where your expertise comes in. To understand standards fully, you must parse them carefully, understanding the cognition called for, the content addressed, and the context in which the standard should be assessed.

Consider this eleventh- and twelfth-grade standard from the *Common Core State Standards for English Language Arts* (National Governors

Association, 2010, p. 40.): "Cite strong and thorough textual evidence to support analysis of what the text says explicitly as well as inferences drawn from the text, including determining where the text leaves matters uncertain." This is a lofty goal, and there are many stepping-stones along the way if a student is to achieve it. For example, students must understand both explicit and implicit information and be able to make valid inferences from a text. Also, the standard is not about regurgitating; it is about analysis. The student must cite evidence in order to analyze a text, not just prove that they have read and comprehended the text. If you and your colleagues wanted to monitor student mastery of this standard, there are several learning targets you'd have to check along the way, such as:

- I understand the differences between implicit and explicit information in a text.
- I can make valid inferences about a text and cite evidence to support my inferences.
- I can identify where a text/author leaves matters uncertain or doesn't fully explain.
- I can analyze text, citing strong, thorough textual evidence.

The process of unpacking and unwrapping a standard to drill down to the learning targets is discussed more thoroughly in Chapter 5, but as you can see from this example, understanding the component parts of any standard is critical not only for your work as an individual, but also for a Data Team's collective efficacy. No teacher can assess well what he or she doesn't understand well.

Understanding what your standards mean is important. Understanding which standards take priority is also important. Educators prioritize their standards so that their curriculum emphasizes those standards that are broader, more all-encompassing, or higher in rigor than others. They also prioritize standards that are heavily tested so that students have a great deal of experience with these before external assessments occur. You and your colleagues are likely working from a set of prioritized standards that either you created yourself or that your school system created with teacher input. Prioritized standards provide the first layer of focus for a Data Team. The other standards don't disappear. As Larry Ainsworth (2013) points out in *Prioritizing the Common Core*, "The supporting standards often become the instructional scaffolds to help students understand and attain the more rigorous and comprehensive priority standards" (p. xv). As your Data Team formatively assesses prioritized standards, properly deconstructed (and reconstructed) as specific learning goals, you steer your students to eventual mastery.

Assessment is another tool for Data Teams to use.

What You Know About Assessment

Depending on when you were trained to be a teacher, you may have had very little coursework (if any at all) on assessing student learning. We find that when we work with educators, there has not been a great deal of on-the-job training with how to assess students fairly and accurately—and it often seems as if this training has been in a "school of hard knocks." One of the best features of a Data Team–powered PLC is that it allows every member of the team to become a savvier assessor, and this benefits students mightily.

In the education world, there are two large categories of assessment, formative and summative. Formative assessment is frequent and comes in many forms, from something as simple as asking students to give a "thumbs up" during a class discussion to something more complex and time-consuming as writing a summary of the content of a chapter. Formative assessments may be in-the-moment checks for understanding, like asking students to hold up a small dry-erase board displaying an answer to a question or orchestrating a think-pair-share so that you can hear students informally discussing content. They may also be more structured and formal, like a bell-ringer assignment that requires students to answer five multiple-choice questions about previously studied content.

Data Teams give common formative assessments (CFAs) that they design to understand student mastery of the learning targets derived from one or more standards. These CFAs may be short or long and may contain items of different formats: selected response (matching, fill-in-the-blank, multiple-choice), short constructed response (lists, diagrams/labels, one or more sentences), long constructed response (paragraphs, essays), and even performance tasks (projects, presentations). The results of these CFAs guide the next steps of the Data Team. Many of the educators with whom we have worked say that formative assessment is "assessment *for* learning" versus "assessment *of* learning," because its express purpose is to help the learner continue toward mastery of a standard.

Summative assessment is evaluative. It is designed to assess learning at the end of a period of instruction and is the basis of reporting grades. Summative assessments may be similar to formatives in their structure and design—but it's their use that distinguishes them. Summative assessments are considered more of an end point than a midpoint (although they don't have to be). Generally, for Data Team work, the team uses short formatives in order to prepare students for an eventual summative, with the goal that as many students as possible do well on the summative.

As an individual teacher, the processes you use for both formative and summative assessment may differ somewhat from what your Data Team does. That's normal. Remember that as a collaborative Data Team member, you will stretch yourself professionally. By taking part in the CFA and resulting data analysis process with your team, you may find ideas and practices that you incorporate into your own teaching beyond what you're doing with your team. You may enhance the full range of formative assessment techniques you use because of what you learn alongside your team. This is one of the best benefits of the Data Team process—that each teacher becomes more masterful in assessing student learning.

The ultimate goal of all assessment is that we as educators can better understand what our students have learned. If we understand, we can respond. If we can remember that, as Data Team members, we seek the optimal response (instead of high scores), we can maximize our collective efficacy.

How students learn best is varied, and as educators, we must be adaptive to meet the needs of all our students.

Dr. Jill Hackett sums up why thoughtful assessment is key to the Data Teams process.

INSIGHTS FROM COLLEAGUES

Dr. Jill Hackett, associate superintendent, Topeka Public School Unified School District No. 501, Topeka, Kansas

Now more than ever with teaching and learning occurring in full remote or hybrid learning modes, it is essential that we have confirmation of what students have learned and what they have yet to learn. John Hattie speaks of the importance of teacher clarity when planning for and delivering instruction. Equally important is the need for clarity of the success criteria for students. Both teaching and learning are greatly enhanced when there is clarity between the teacher and students regarding the purpose of the lesson and the agreed upon evidence of success.

When lessons are collaboratively designed based on standards, with the interests and intellectual needs of students in mind, there is a much higher likelihood of students learning successfully. It is through common formative assessments that we can determine, with clarity, what students learned or have yet to learn.

Working together to develop rigorous and engaging lessons with clarity of instructional intent, and clarity of success criteria as revealed in formative assessment data, is essential for effective teaching and learning to occur. What do I want students to learn? How will I know if they learned it? And then how will I use the data to make the next instructional decision?

What You Know About How Students Learn Best

Whether you're a first-year teacher or a veteran of many years in the classroom, you have probably learned a great deal about how students learn. You have also most likely learned that not every technique you use as a teacher works for every student. There is wide variability in the amount of support and practices students need for something to "click."

Data Teams constantly ask themselves, "What must students master as a result of our teaching?" They work on adjusting their teaching continuously so that as many students as possible master the standards.

Data Team work is first and foremost about continuously improving core instruction. Quality core instruction framed by a guaranteed, viable curriculum ensures access, equity, and opportunity. When a team administers a CFA, it includes all the students represented by the team members. Then, depending on what the data indicates and on what the team decides to do in response, there are many options for addressing student learning needs. Teachers may come up with differentiation options to orchestrate within their own classrooms. They may devise cooperative learning with groups structured by levels of current proficiency. Students may be regrouped, and time may be redistributed so that students who weren't successful in core instruction receive something different from what they received before. There are so many options that we have seen Data Teams utilize, but at their core, all these responses take into account how students learn best.

As Sarah Sparks (2013) notes, "Students' ability to learn depends not just on the quality of their textbooks and teachers, but also on the comfort and safety they feel at school and the strength of their relationships with adults and peers there" (p. 1). Over the years, many Data Teams we've supported find that students (particularly secondary students) appreciate that their teachers are meeting with their colleagues to improve their own instruction. Relationships with students are strengthened when students realize their teachers are looking at their work not only to generate grades and keep students busy, but also to find new, innovative ways to support students. Teachers who seek to cultivate and sustain a growth mindset in their students exemplify that mindset as part of a team that works constantly to improve teaching and learning.

Students need feedback that they can understand so they can move forward in their learning. Effective feedback is goal-referenced, specific, useful, and actionable (Wiggins, 2012). Writing comments like "Good job!" and "Nice work" on student papers is insufficient. Letter grades or rubric scores may be insufficient as well if the learner doesn't understand specifically what to do more of, what to do less of, or what to do differently next time. In the Data Team process, as teachers clarify with each other what they see in student work and make inferences about root causes, they collectively figure out how to give students the much-needed, specific feedback that makes a real difference.

Lastly, students also respond to some instructional strategies better than others. Robert Marzano and John Hattie have both contributed greatly to the field with their syntheses of effective instructional strategies. Many teachers know from the work of those two scholars that strategies like summarizing, note-taking, the jigsaw method, mnemonics, and reciprocal teaching are powerful when used with students. These few strategies are just some of the very many that a Data Team can consider employing in response to evidence of student learning. A spirit of innovation should buoy your team at step four of the Data Team process (and will be discussed more thoroughly in Chapter 5).

Daniel Scott speaks to how important it is for us to use the data collected to move each student forward.

INSIGHTS FROM COLLEAGUES

Daniel Scott, instructional coach, Warsaw Community Schools, Warsaw, Indiana

We have traditionally hoped that students would follow directions, complete what is required, and move on. Yet, questions have lingered without being asked. Do the students genuinely understand what they are learning? How do we know? How and why do the students think that they know? Will this learning extend beyond the test they just finished? Is this evidence actually *evidence*? These shaded-in bubbles will only go so far for us all if we are to help this world and the institution in place progress out of systems too long unexamined. We as collective learners (educators, students, and others) must look at the evidence of learning students are being challenged with.

When evidence of learning is collected, it provides us with a chance to uncover and discover deeper elements about our students and ourselves. These elements may look different for educators based on their life experiences, education, biases, etc. Meanwhile, individual students as well as groups of them will hopefully be encouraged to strive for innovation, creativity, and collaboration that defy standardized assessments. This adds another piece to the puzzle of student learning that teachers must consider. The evidence we gather of student learning will not be a one-size-fits-all answer filled out in a bubble that is scanned to tell us how "smart" a child is. It is to be project-based, solution-focused with real-world problems (that cross subjects agreed upon over a century ago) to allow empathy and compassion to drive ways that students can reflect on and contribute to their local or global community.

When students are ready for the next steps, teachers can guide them into the internal territory of self-assessment. This arena not only examines academic work but also the heart, collaboration, and soft skills that will exceed our expectations. That said, yes, we are assessing *for* learning at this time while also considering how learning will take place as they grow into adults. How will students know what evidence will show their learning when they leave the classroom, building, and institution? We as educators are in the business of changing lives and having faith that we will do so through applying what is best. How and why we gather evidence of our student learning is a critical part of moving forward.

Through the collection and evaluation of information by the Data Team, the intended result is the progression of all students.

How the Data Team Process Helps Every Student Progress

Teachers are responsible for the learning of every single student with whom they connect. In recent years, this basic tenet of education has come under additional scrutiny and is also the focus of major legislation. Data Team work helps teachers collectively meet the needs of all students.

Multi-tiered systems of support (MTSS) are mentioned in the Every Student Succeeds Act (ESSA) of 2015 and are an important concept as related to Data Teams. And while the purpose of Data Teams is not specifically to manage a school's MTSS, Data Team meetings can help teams better serve students who are not making expected progress.

Most MTSS systems operate within a three-tiered structure, with tier one usually called "core instruction." High-quality, core instruction is fundamental to the Data Teams process. As teachers become more comfortable and more expert in the Data Teams process, core instruction—that is, the whole-group lessons that all students have access to—is strengthened. Teachers employ new instructional strategies and create different grouping patterns. They use technology in novel ways. They engage in continuous dialogue with other members of their Data Team and tweak what they are doing from day to day or class period to class period. Thus, students are better served in tier one, leading to fewer students needing interventions and other specialized services.

MTSS, of course, requires more than just excellent core instruction. Tier two services, often called "targeted supports," are made available to some students based on their lack of sufficient progress. Tier two differs from core instruction in that it is offered in smaller groups (usually within the main classroom) and focuses on remediation acceleration of deficient skills. Tier three offers even greater intensity, with students being placed in very small groups or receiving one-on-one support, and lasts for a longer period of time than tier two. Often, interventionists and other specialists deliver tier three instruction.

It is important to remember that Data Teams focus on what can be done within the control of the team. Excellent core instruction is fully in control of each teacher and should be the focus of much of what occurs in Data Team meetings. Tier two configurations and methods are also within the control of each teacher. Data Teams often create highly effective tier two supports. As the saying goes, two heads (or more than two!) are better than one.

MTSS also requires the monitoring of progress as students are served in tiers two and three. Again, while the work of progress monitoring is not the core function of the Data Teams process, the two processes must inform each other. All the while that tier two and three supports are transpiring, excellent core instruction still occurs for the entire range of students the particular Data Team serves, and the Data Teams process continues. Tier two and tier three interventions do not supplant core instruction but complement it. Likewise, MTSS complements the Data Teams process—it does not supplant it.

Ajit Pethe experienced dramatic improvement when implementing Data Teams at his school when he was an elementary principal. Every child's growth was important.

INSIGHTS FROM COLLEAGUES

Ajit Pethe, chief of schools, Jefferson Parish, Louisiana

When I was principal at Luling Elementary in St. Charles Parish, Louisiana, we implemented Data Teams to address our results in math.

After hitting roadblock after roadblock, the third-grade teachers at Luling Elementary were unsure how to help their students understand the concept of rounding numbers. Despite attempting a variety of instructional strategies, nothing seemed to help strengthen our students' understanding. After closely analyzing student errors and misconceptions, the third-grade teachers came to the realization that their students were unsuccessful because they lacked the strong foundation in number sense needed to proceed.

Our assistant superintendent began a Data Teams study group, including representatives from our school. Intrigued by what we were learning, several representatives from our district attended various events offered by HMH/ICLE. We decided to implement the Data Teams process at our school, focusing on third-grade math outcomes. Additionally, we formed a building-level team consisting of representatives from each grade at our school. This team became the team that later grew Data Teams throughout the grade levels and subject areas.

Prior to experiencing the benefits firsthand, my team and I were skeptical about the Data Teams comparison of pre- and post-test data. Our belief was that any teacher should be able to take the results of a pre-test, implement a strategy to address challenge areas, and then show growth on a post-test. What we failed to realize is the importance of everything that takes place in between the pre- and post-test. It was only as a result of each teacher's actions that significant improvements were made, and each teacher grew as

(Continued)

part of the collaborative team. Teachers focused on the specific misconceptions of their students. Students were no longer simply gaining a surface-level understanding before the teacher moved on to the next concept, but were more deeply applying concepts.

Teachers benefited professionally from the dialogue in Data Team meetings and from professional development they engaged in as they continued in the Data Team process. The Data Team process had a huge impact on student achievement, resulting in higher math achievement and our school improving its state performance score from 75.1 to 102.3, exceeding expectations.

Students benefited in many ways. Before, our students did not have a clear vision of themselves as learners and scholars. They had not set academic goals for themselves, nor had they been encouraged to set them. Our students' thinking was transformed by the Data Teams process. Students came each day focused on meeting or exceeding their short-term goals. They held their teachers accountable by asking for and expecting feedback on their work. The school became a place where both students and teachers sought continuous improvement.

The work of Data Teams truly brings out the best in formative assessment. Individual teachers grow in assessing more accurately and fairly, and teams learn how to assess what's most important, often in innovative ways. As teams become increasingly effective, they respond to students in ways that allow students to reach their full learning potential while providing necessary supports along the way.

QUESTIONS TO CONSIDER

1. How well do I know the standards I'm required to teach? How well does my Data Team understand the standards that we're collectively assessing?
2. What instructional strategies has my Data Team used with success?
3. What instructional strategies would I like to find out more about so that I can share information with my team?

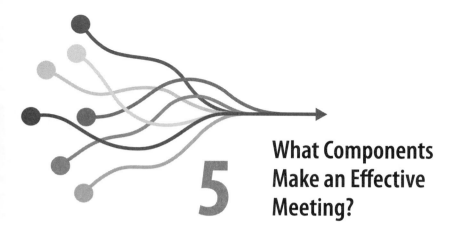

5 What Components Make an Effective Meeting?

The right kind of continuous, structured teacher collaboration improves the quality of teaching and pays big, often immediate, dividends in student learning and professional morale in virtually any setting.
—Mike Schmoker, *Results Now*

The publication of *Professional Learning Communities at Work: Best Practices for Enhancing Student Achievement* by Richard DuFour and Robert Eaker in 1998 ignited new interest in schools operating as true learning organizations. Richard and Rebecca DuFour and their colleagues have since published other books and numerous articles about the PLC (professional learning community) concept. According to this influential, original book, when a school is a true PLC, its members collectively pursue a shared mission and shared goals. They work interdependently in teams that are focused on student learning. They engage in collective inquiry into best practice. As a result of their inquiry, they innovate to continuously improve student achievement.

If professional learning communities are the "what" of school improvement, then the practices of Data Teams serve as the "how." The five-step process that Data Teams use in their meetings, discussed later in this chapter, along with monitoring the effectiveness of selected innovations, provides a flexible framework in which educators can begin to operate as a learning community.

The process described in this chapter is one which scores of Data Teams have used, benefiting thousands of students. The process is rooted in collecting data and collaboratively examining it to continuously improve instruction.

Gathering Data That's Useful

Too often Data Teams begin with a careful analysis of large-scale, external data (such as state or system standardized test data). *This is not the kind of data that effective teams continue to examine.* Data Teams examine data derived from frequent, common, teacher-created, formative assessments, which are administered to all the students represented by the teachers on the team.

These common formative assessments (CFAs) are created from the unpacked, prioritized standards. Ideally, the team collaboratively develops each CFA. We have seen some teams rotate the duty of drafting a CFA among team members, but without collaboratively critiquing and revising these drafts, they don't always work well. Assessments differ in both format and quality when their creation rotates among members rather than being a collaborative process.

The team should begin by selecting one or a handful of prioritized standards to assess. After each team determines the specific learning targets for which they will collect data, they must create the CFA that will elicit evidence about student proficiency.

Assessment Design

Teacher-created CFAs may consist of entirely original items or of items available through sources like online databases and ancillary materials, or of a combination of original and nonoriginal items. However, it's critical that the team agrees that the items on the assessment accurately measure the learning targets from the unwrapped standards. Some teams we have worked with over the years have student management software that tracks each student's progress standard by standard, so it is very important that if such a program exists in your school, you and your team ensure that each item on a CFA is indeed an accurate measure of what is being tested.

Aside from electronic tracking of mastery of learning targets and standards, there is the concept of test item validity. An item is only valid if it actually measures what the team says it measures and what is actually intended by the standard. For example, if the standard is about citing textual evidence, and the students are asked only to sort relevant and irrelevant evidence related to a position stated in a text they just read, they have not cited evidence. They have only taken evidence presented to them and judged it as supportive or not. This is why unpacking standards all the way down to the level of specific learning targets is critical. Understanding relevant and irrelevant evidence is certainly a step in the learning progression toward mastery of the citing evidence standard, but it is not representative of the entire standard.

As the Data Team starts to design a CFA, all members should agree on what constitutes a correct, complete answer for each item and what overall proficiency is for the CFA. For example, an assessment about specific, grade-level writing conventions might include five multiple-choice questions that ask students to correct errors in the given sentences. The assessment might also include a short, constructed-response item for which students must write several complete, correct sentences on a familiar topic. Overall proficiency (or "meeting standard") for this assessment could consist of a student getting at least four of the multiple-choice items correct, in addition to scoring proficient (on a rubric or scale) on the constructed-response item. In this scenario, the team should collaboratively select or create the sentences for the multiple-choice items, create the correct multiple-choice answers and plausible distractors, write the constructed-response item, and design the rubric or scale to score the constructed-response item. We also usually recommend that teams write a sample answer to constructed-response items prior to giving CFAs. This allows for team members to experience the question from the students' perspective. It also helps the team come to agreement about what each level of the rubric means before using the rubric for scoring.

The scheduling of the assessments is the next step.

Scheduling the Assessments

Some Data Teams work in schools or systems that require both pre- and post-assessments for each unit or marking period. The pre-assessment is given prior to significant instruction so that teachers can ascertain where students stand before the unit proceeds. Many of these assessments we've seen assess prior knowledge, prerequisite skills, and academic vocabulary. Some of them also include items based on new skills and knowledge that are forthcoming in the unit. These items are included so that if some students already demonstrate mastery, they can be accelerated. A post-assessment is often more summative in nature and measures only the new learning that was acquired in the unit.

Some Data Teams work more on a rolling schedule during which they assess certain learning targets repeatedly instead of using a true pre- and post-process. These teams may select a group of learning targets that covers a time span of a few week. They begin by assessing the first (or first few) learning targets. They continue by assessing the next handful, and so on, until all the learning targets for the selected, prioritized standards have been fully covered.

In another adaptation of the rolling process, some teams assess the learning targets for only one or two critical standards for a few months or even an entire semester. For example, one small, rural high school we worked with for over two years assessed citing evidence and determining central idea for informational texts every few weeks school-wide. This went on for three months until about 70 percent of the entire student body showed mastery. Then they switched their focus school-wide to the skill of citing evidence and determining theme for literary texts or passages. They worked on this for about two months until about 70 percent of the student body showed mastery. Then, as the dates for state testing rapidly approached, they gave CFAs every two weeks that paired informational and literary texts. What did they assess on these CFAs? Citing evidence, determining central idea, determining theme, and comparing and contrasting the texts. The entire faculty (about ten teachers) was a Data Team and collaborated to unpack the standards, create the CFAs, administer the CFAs, and determine their response.

Yet other teams have "standing" CFAs. For example, a group of U.S. history teachers uses a document-based question (DBQ) every seven to ten days as their CFA. They do these standing assignments all year long. These DBQs may or may not be directly aligned with the current course content for each teacher, so they don't require that students use new knowledge to answer them. Instead, they assess critical skills like close reading, inferring, and citing textual evidence. This particular team felt that assessing these crucial social science skills frequently would serve them and their students well. They also give summative assessments that are very content-focused, such as unit tests, midterm exams, and final exams.

Other teams use in-class assignments such as bell ringers or exit tickets as their CFAs. The type and frequency of CFAs should be driven by dialogue with your team as you all keep in mind the kind of evidence you need to help you accurately determine where each student is along the learning progression for any given standard. There really is no "one-size-fits-all" when it comes to CFAs.

Overall, it's crucial to stay focused on the learning targets that are truly most important. In the past few years of working with Data Teams, we have found that the reading standards about citing evidence, central idea, theme, and author's purpose are the most common ones that English language arts teams assess with success. In contrast, ELA teams that choose to assess minutiae like comma placement or types of clauses do not see appreciable gains either on their own assessments or state tests. Many social studies/history teams we have worked with assess reading and writing skills that apply to their content versus declarative knowledge like names and dates on their CFAs. Many math and science teams we have worked with assess a mixture of declarative content knowledge and application of skills on their CFAs.

There are many choices about what to focus on in terms of the standards and learning targets selected. There are also many choices for how to design and administer CFAs. Part of the beauty of collaboration is that you and your team will find what works best, and along the way, you'll learn a great deal about formative assessment practices.

Assessments won't necessarily be of the best quality initially in a Data Team's work; however, it is critical that teams start assessing student learning immediately after they are formed. The information gained from common assessments, even if not "perfect," can be acted upon quickly so that student learning is increased. There's no time to waste! Don't let perfection be the enemy of the good; get out there and get busy.

Let's looks at what it takes to create a CFA.

Creating the CFA, Start to Finish

If you and your Data Team are ready to start meeting, first you must create the tool that will give you information you need: the CFA. Briefly, the process includes the following:

1. *Select one or more prioritized standards.* We generally recommend that you select no more than three standards so that the CFA can

be administered and scored quickly. If you're doing a pre- and post-design that covers an entire unit or marking period, you may have to select more than three standards.

2. *Unwrap or unpack the standards.* There are several ways to unpack your identified standards; we recommend these steps first proposed by Larry Ainsworth (2003):
   - Circle the words that depict skills or that students need to know and be able to do. These are verbs.
   - Underline the words that depict content—both facts and concepts. These are nouns and noun phrases.
   - Working from the circled and underlined words, organize them in a chart or other visual that makes sense to you and your team. This is a concise representation of the standard.
   - Consider the level of rigor that the standard represents. Most districts we work with refer to either Bloom's Taxonomy of Educational Objectives (Anderson and Krathwohl, 2001) or Webb's Depth of Knowledge (2005) at this step.

3. *Write learning targets.* Consider all the stated and implied learning targets that this unpacked standard represents and the level of rigor you identified. Create a series of learning targets that make clear how the student reaches mastery of the full standard. These can be written as student-friendly "I can" statements if your team wishes or if your school or district requires this format.

4. *Determine what kinds of items and how many items you'll need.* Many teams use a combination of selected-response items (multiple-choice, true-false, matching) and constructed-response items. Your team will have to discuss how many items you need for each learning target to feel comfortable that a student is proficient. You will also have to create any rubric or scale you need to score a constructed-response item.

5. *Draft the CFA.* Ensure that directions are clear, that items are worded correctly, and that there is room for students to write if necessary.

How you and your team will work together is a critical part of the process. Everyone must be on the same page and agree to the team norms and expectations for it to be a successful collaboration.

Meeting Before Data Is Collected

When Data Teams are first established, each team must determine and agree to its own norms. In other words, how will they work together as a team? The norms are the behavioral expectations or "rules" that will be adhered to during meetings. Many teams establish norms such as the following:

- Arrive for the meeting on time, with all needed materials.
- Stay on topic.
- Use active listening when others are speaking.
- Adhere to the times established in the agenda.
- Reflect on your own practice and share ideas that move the group forward.
- Express concerns about the team's work in the meetings, not to others outside of the meetings who aren't on the team.
- Complete tasks as assigned.
- Once you commit to a strategy or other action in the team meeting, implement it.
- Celebrate the team's successes.

We have seen highly effective teams whose norms are even more specific than those above. For example, what does it mean to be on time? Does it mean that everyone is at the table at a certain time, or does it mean that they arrive within a window of time that allows them to use the restroom or grab a cup of coffee? We have also seen teams that make the expectations for participation and attention clearer by asking everyone to put their cell phones in a basket or face-down in the center of the table during the meeting. These simple tricks help all members stay focused.

Effective Data Team leaders sometimes stop meetings if norms are violated and process the issue with the team. When this happens, norms may be reviewed to ensure understanding or adjusted for future meetings if the team so agrees.

If leaders want to collect formative data about the Data Teams process in a school, they can ask questions like the following to better understand norms and how those norms are supporting collaboration:

- How often does your Data Team meeting start and end on time?
- How often do all members of your Data Team come prepared for the work that needs to be done?

- How well do you understand the Data Teams process?
- How well do you understand your role and responsibilities on the Data Team?
- In Data Team meetings, are your contributions valued? How do you know?
- In Data Team meetings, are the contributions of all team members valued?

All members of a Data Team have joint responsibility for the effectiveness of the meetings that are held. Therefore, it is important that each Data Team spend time up front (prior to designing assessments and prior to conducting before- and after-instruction meetings) developing norms for the team's work.

Meeting After Data Is Collected

Data Teams meet to act on what is revealed from a common formative assessment. Briefly, the following five steps comprise the work that happens at those meetings. These steps will be discussed in more depth in the section that follows.

1. *Collect and chart the data.* Members examine the number and percentage of students proficient and nonproficient both teacher by teacher and for the entire team. They may also drill down into the data to increase clarity about exactly which students are struggling, which are close to proficient already, and which may need acceleration because they are at or beyond proficiency. If there are subgroups that the team, school, or school system is focusing on, the team may also examine the data for those subgroups.

2. *Analyze the data and prioritize needs.* The analysis should focus on urgent needs inferred from the evidence. Team members should ask themselves, "Why are students performing the way they are?" Inferring root cause is critical because later in the meeting, team members must target specific learning needs and match instructional strategies to those needs *so that the highest number of students possible will achieve proficiency.*

3. *Set a short-term SMART goal.* SMART stands for **s**pecific, **mea**surable, **a**chievable, **r**elevant, and **t**ime-oriented. This goal is the growth target and clearly states the expected percentage of students who will be proficient and higher in the measured standards at the end of the designated instructional time. Generally, achievement of the goal is expected at the end of an instructional unit (or after four to six weeks of instruction). While some teams set quarterly goals, the most successful teams we have worked with look at a shorter time frame.

4. *Determine instructional strategies to implement to raise student proficiency.* The team should ask, "Which strategies will have the greatest impact on student learning based on the needs and root causes that we identified?" Another question that often deserves discussion is "What strategies are individual teachers implementing with a high degree of success, and should these practices be replicated?" The important thing to remember about this step is that at least one research-based, high-yield instructional strategy must be agreed upon and immediately implemented in order to enhance student learning.

5. *Determine results indicators.* Basically, results indicators state the evidence that the agreed-upon strategies are being implemented effectively and having the desired effects. Results indicators describe the teacher and student behaviors that will be seen as the strategies are implemented.

It should be clear that steps one and three are related, as are steps two and four (see Figure 5.1). Understanding the current level of mastery, based on data collected in step one, is critical as the team determines a reasonable, short-term goal in step three. The learning needs discovered in step two must be linked directly to the instructional strategies considered in step four. Instructional strategies don't apply randomly; they must be selected because they have the potential to greatly impact the urgent needs inferred from student work.

Meeting often is the key to success. Data Teams also often meet when there is no new data from a CFA to review. During these meetings, team members usually discuss how the implementation of their instructional strategies is going. They may also bring examples of student work to offer

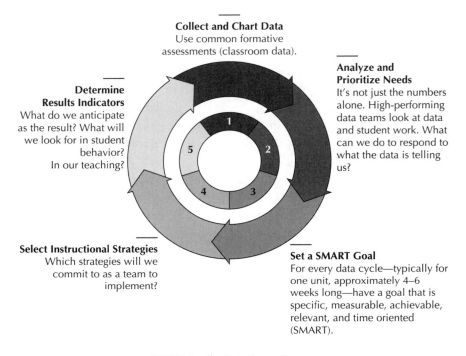

Collect and Chart Data
Use common formative
assessments (classroom data).

**Analyze and
Prioritize Needs**
It's not just the numbers
alone. High-performing
data teams look at data
and student work. What
can we do to respond to
what the data is telling
us?

**Determine
Results Indicators**
What do we anticipate
as the result? What will
we look for in student
behavior?
In our teaching?

Select Instructional Strategies
Which strategies will we
commit to as a team to
implement?

Set a SMART Goal
For every data cycle—typically for
one unit, approximately 4–6
weeks long—have a goal that is
specific, measurable, achievable,
relevant, and time oriented
(SMART).

FIGURE 5.1   The Data Teams Process

for collegial analysis. If there is not new CFA data to examine, there is plenty
to talk about related to steps four and five. The following questions can
guide those types of meetings:

- Are our selected instructional strategies working as intended? If not,
  how might we adjust?
- Are there instructional strategies we should add?
- What evidence are students showing us that they are moving closer to
  proficiency and mastery?
- Are there specific students who need targeted assistance because they're
  not making progress yet?

Successful meetings depend on the adults and how they engage with
each other, as we covered in Chapter 2. Data Team meetings are most effective when people play specific roles as they work through the steps just
described.

Roles People Play in Meetings

Every Data Team needs a leader and members. There are several types of responsibilities that team members can take on. These responsibilities are often determined based on the size of the team and the strengths of the members—but regardless of these factors, and others that may be in play, several key responsibilities must be met at all times in order for a team to function effectively.

The one role that must be filled is the Data Team leader. This person can volunteer for the role, be appointed by the principal, or be selected by the team. This role may also rotate among members, but if it does rotate, all members of the team must be well-equipped to serve.

The Data Team leader must be both a good listener and an effective facilitator of dialogue. He or she is not necessarily a person who fills another leadership role (like department chairperson or grade-level team leader). In many cases, the teachers who fill those roles already have many demands on their time, so they may not be a good fit—or some of their other obligations will need to be reduced.

Data Team leaders are not pseudo-administrators, meaning that they do not evaluate the performance of colleagues or supervise those colleagues in any way. It is important that all members of a Data Team (and the principal) understand the leader is primarily a facilitator, not an evaluator in any sense of the word.

Data Team leaders must sincerely believe that all students can achieve at high levels with the appropriate support from adults. They must also be willing to challenge the views and assumptions of their colleagues to strategize and innovate so that all students experience academic success. Because they serve as leaders in innovation, they should be well-informed about instructional strategies. Often principals and central office administrators target Data Team leaders to attend conferences and engage in other forms of professional development so that they can serve as knowledgeable resources for their colleagues.

Other roles we have seen used well include recorder, data technician, data wall curator, timekeeper, and focus monitor. The recorder takes notes at the meeting and disseminates them to the entire team and the administration. The data technician collects data and prepares it for sharing with the team. A data wall curator is charged with displaying the ongoing results within the school. A timekeeper monitors the time that each step takes at the meeting and helps to ensure the team has time to complete the entire process. The focus monitor works with the timekeeper to ensure that dialogue stays tightly focused on teaching and learning.

All members of the team must play the crucial role of engaged participant. While it is generally up to the leader to set the agenda, communicate the meeting time and place to everyone, and facilitate the discussion, each person must make meaningful contributions and commit to the strategies once those strategies are determined.

Team members should also be prepared to listen respectfully, pose questions to push the group's thinking forward, and take on portions of the group's work, like maintaining Data Team records, making copies of the common assessment, and researching research-based instructional strategies.

As with most teams and task forces in schools, Data Teams should create a set of norms that guides their work. Roles and responsibilities are often covered in a good set of norms.

We gave a snapshot above of the five steps you and your team should follow. Let's go into more detail on each.

A Closer Look at the Five Steps

Let's look at the five steps that Data Teams follow when there is new assessment information in more detail. It should be noted that even though there are suggestions for how to conduct each step, teams should make the steps their own. Dr. Ken Oertling, a former high school principal, speaks to that.

INSIGHT FROM COLLEAGUES

Dr. Ken Oertling, superintendent, St. Charles Parish Public Schools, Louisiana

Using Data Teams increased student achievement across six different subject areas at Hahnville High School because of teacher collaboration, use of formative assessment data to drive instruction and support, and the flexible use of the Data Teams' process steps. No one team during my six years as principal ever used each step in the same manner. While most teams started using them in a prescribed way, as more cycles passed and collaboration centered on teacher effectiveness and student support, most of them modified and adjusted their steps to meet the needs of the team. The modifications of steps were necessary for each team's growth and to address the varying levels of skill development and content mastery in different courses. Those teams that modified the steps to meet the needs of the team produced better student achievement results than those less inclined to move past the standard step-by-step approach.

Step One: Collect and Chart the Data

In step one in a typical Data Team meeting, the team members examine data in preparation for the focused instruction that will come or post-assessment data to determine if the desired student learning goals were met. This step requires teachers to collaborate around a set of data from a CFA. The data can be sent to the team's data technician prior to the meeting so that it is assembled and ready to view when the meeting begins, or the team may process and chart the data on the spot, with each person reporting in turn until all data is shared.

Teams not yet proficient in step one may spend time criticizing the assessment itself or particular items that appear on it, thus taking valuable time away from digging deeper into the students' responses. Even on assessments that are flawed in design, valuable information about student learning resides in the answers. These teams may also have one or more members who do not report their data. This can occur for various reasons. The member may not have finished scoring the work when the meeting occurs or may have been absent and not had time to score. Obviously, this situation must be remedied if the team is to function well, because without current information about the learning of all students represented by the team, the best instructional strategy remedies cannot be determined.

Whatever the reason for incomplete data, the team should not wait. Waiting for someone or their data can force the meeting agenda to run too long, and it is vital that plenty of time be reserved for the discussion in steps four and five. Teams must operate with the information they have at hand, on time. The Data Team must make inferences and generate hypotheses about how to raise student achievement based on the information they have. If their strategies do not prove as effective as they had predicted, then the team can collectively determine its next steps. The team should not be paralyzed into inaction because of incomplete data. However, in the long run, teams must find ways to ensure they have both timely and complete data so that their actions become increasingly targeted to the students' most urgent learning needs.

High-performing teams learn to complete step one in just a few minutes, saving precious time for the analysis of student work that comes at step two. They quickly and accurately chart or report the number of students that actually took the assessment. They then divide student performance into several meaningful predetermined categories. Often, these categories include the number and names of students who are proficient and higher, those who are predicted to be proficient after instructional strategies are applied, those who need targeted instruction or additional time to meet the standard, and those who require intensive interventions.

If multiple prioritized standards or learning goals were covered on any given assessment, the data is ideally displayed in a form that makes it clear what the levels of student proficiency are for each standard or objective. When Data Teams first begin working, they may choose to design assessments based on only one prioritized standard or expected learning goal to provide both brevity and clarity. However, as teams increase in their sophistication, they often design assessments that focus on multiple prioritized standards or expected learning goals—or assessments that blend "old" items with new, effectively checking to see if previous learning has been retained.

Finally, smoothly running teams translate the numbers of students in each performance level into percentages that will help the team establish one or more SMART goals in step three. It is important to use percentages to get a more global view of the entire group of students that the team is responsible for. Using raw numbers can be misleading or problematic in some cases because of student transiency, student absenteeism, or school events or disruptions. Focusing on the individual students in each proficiency level is helpful as a micro view, but viewing overall percentages is also helpful as a macro view. Both views work in harmony to inform the team.

Figure 5.2 is an example of how one team displayed its data for step one. This particular team lists only the names of students who are proficient or higher and those of the ones who are already in need of intensive assistance

Teacher Names	Number of Students Assessed	Number and/ or Names of Students Who Are Proficient and Higher	Number and/ or Names of Students Who Will Likely Be Proficient after Instruction	Number and/ or Names of Students in Need of Targeted Instruction or Additional Time	Number and/ or Names of Students in Need of Extensive Intervention
Gregg	24	4 Michelle, Katie, Andrea, Jordan	5	10	5 Jada, Eileen, Tomas, Deke, Isaiah
Lassiter	20	0	5	5	10 Linda, Juan, Tracey, Mike, Cathy, Doug, Larry, Cecilia, Paul, Jillian
Cordova	28	3 Austin, Carla, Cedric	7	13	5 Tony, Laura, Emily, Howie, Jake
Total	72	10%	24%	38%	28%

FIGURE 5.2　Example of Step One, Data Reporting

so that the team can keep these students foremost in their minds as they determine next steps. The single standard addressed on this pre-assessment example was about students being able to make valid inferences when reading on-grade-level, informational text.

Data can be further disaggregated into subgroups if desired. Also, individual students whose progress is being monitored as part of a multi-tiered system of support (MTSS) process can be highlighted. One benefit to deeper data analysis via disaggregation is that additional school-based academic services may be identified for students in all the nonproficient categories. Remember that the team's primary goal is to make changes in their own instructional practice as a result of better understanding the learning needs of their students—but if they are able to secure additional, out-of-classroom assistance for nonproficient students, this kind of support can work very well in tandem with improved core instruction.

Step Two: Analyze Data and Prioritize Needs

In this step, the team analyzes student work from a CFA to identify the strengths students display in addition to their most urgent learning needs. Their most urgent learning needs become the focus for future changes in instruction. When student work samples are examined closely, even subtle differences in performance can teach educators a great deal, not only about the students but about the teaching behind the performance.

In this second step, teams must go beyond simply labeling what is "right" and "wrong." They must ask themselves *why* students are performing the way they are. Some teams devolve into discussing challenges that are beyond a teacher's direct control, such as the following:

- The students didn't learn the concept or skill in the previous grade level or course;
- The students don't do their homework;
- The students are often tardy or absent; or
- The students' home situation prevents them from doing well at school.

Knowing the above factors is important to understanding students' whole story, but discussion of them is not for Data Team meeting time. Discussing things beyond the team's control is unproductive. If you hear comments like the ones listed above, do your part to steer the conversation back to the student work and what it seems to be telling you. Make inferences based on the work and look toward the future, thinking about how you can directly impact student learning for the better.

Some teams struggle with prioritizing students' learning needs. They may end up with several academic needs that all seem equally pressing. Thus, they are unable to enter the discussion of instructional strategies with a clear focus or simply become overwhelmed because all the needs seem urgent. Focus on only one urgent need at step one if the needs seem overwhelming, and use that one need as the basis of your SMART goal in step three.

At step two, the team needs to discuss what they see in the student work as specifically as possible. For example, a math team discovered that students were weak in solving equations with one variable. They asked themselves the following:

- Do students understand what a variable represents? Where is the evidence that tells us this?
- When students isolate the variable, do they remember to do an equivalent operation to the other side of the equation? How often do students forget to do this?
- Are students making copying mistakes when isolating the variable and "bringing it down"?
- Do students label their answer when necessary? If not, why not?

The determination of strategies to employ later in the meeting depends on teams asking and answering questions like these. Simple copying errors would be addressed quite differently during instruction than errors about equivalence.

At step two, effective teams search for the root causes of students' incorrect responses and also look deeply into students' correct answers for clues about how to take them to higher performance levels. When discussing student needs, they prioritize to be most strategic or to get the biggest "bang for the buck" in instruction. To continue with the earlier math team example, understanding what a variable represents and remembering to perform equivalent operations on each side of an equation are far more important conceptually than not bringing a term down correctly or not labeling one's final answer.

In this step, teams can also categorize students into several levels of performance and prioritize needs differently for each group—depending, of course, on what they find in the student work. Sometimes students who are close to proficiency and those who are a little further away have similar confusions, inaccuracies, or limited understandings.

The minutes of one proficient team, seen in Figure 5.3, reflect effective discussion of what the students who are close to reaching proficiency know and can do. This excerpt also reflects numerous valid inferences made from the close examination of student work. (The assessment task was for students to write an accurate summary paragraph after reading a short, on-grade-level informational text.)

High-functioning teams take their analysis at step two even further, prioritizing the students' learning needs to reflect areas that not only impact

Notes About Student Performance	Our Inferences
Strengths: *What do proficient students know, and what can they do proficiently?* • They were able to determine what was important. • They pulled specific content from question. • They used specific examples or supporting details (at least three). • Mechanics like spelling were not distracting. • They used transitions between sentences.	• They know to base their answer specifically on the question that has been posed. • They have been taught about organization of a paragraph: topic sentence, several details, conclusion sentence. • Students who are proficient readers and write like real writers, use correct mechanics and transitions to move the reader along.
Challenges: *What do students struggle with, misunderstand, or need help with?* • They included everything from the original text vs. focusing on the most important details. • Their sense of sentence structure or variety was weak; many sentences start the same way or are structured alike. • Their sense of mechanics is below grade level, especially in punctuation. • Their summary was written in a structure more like a think-aloud than in any certain order.	• They might not know what *summary* means—that it focuses only on important information. • They are not sure how to determine importance of details and to weed out those that don't need to be in a summary. • They need help in structuring and punctuating various types of sentences correctly.

Prioritized Needs:
• Students need to know what *summary* means and see models of proficient summary paragraphs.
• Students need to understand sentence and paragraph structure better.

FIGURE 5.3   Example of Step Two, Analyzing Student Work

the standard or topic at hand, but also have a large impact across standards, topics, and even disciplines. In the math team example, this might mean discussing terms like *equal, equation, equivalence, variable,* and *balance* in a broader context, helping students connect these terms to other disciplines. Numerous researchers (Graves, 2005; Marzano, 2004) have documented that a focus on academic vocabulary benefits students in math class and beyond, so a team that would integrate this focus would be impacting much more than just the students' understanding of equations.

High-functioning teams are particularly expert in prioritizing the needs for the group of students that requires intensive intervention. The teachers spend time figuring out what this group of students is lacking as far as prerequisite skills and knowledge as they search for root causes. They then create a hierarchy of needs so that all assistance given to the identified students is focused on what will help the students the most, the soonest. In other words, they think more in terms of acceleration rather than remediation—which is critical for this group of students because they often are deficient in many skills and lack important conceptual knowledge. If the most important learning needs aren't addressed fast and well for these students, they continue to slip behind.

Step Three: Set a Short-Term SMART Goal

This third step is all about setting a short-term goal that can be reached in a brief instructional cycle (generally one week to one month). Working toward a SMART goal helps focus a team so that their analysis of what students need turns into measurable adult actions. The goal-setting step promotes team accountability and commitment to improved student learning.

When setting, reviewing, or revising a goal in step three, the team should revisit the percentages reported in step one. The students who are close to proficiency and those who are further away but not in need of intensive intervention should all be considered when setting the SMART goal.

Some teams prefer to take a safe route and simply calculate what the total percentage of proficient students would be if every student from the close to proficient category moved to proficient at the end of the instruction cycle. This is an acceptable path. Other teams, however, consider close to proficient students in addition to some or all students in the next category down. Some teams even prefer to take a bold route and set a very high goal because they feel the targeted learning is important enough to have as many students as possible master it. These teams often set goals to have 75 or 80 percent or more of their students reaching proficiency. While an 80 percent proficiency level might seem daunting at first, remember that if the team falls short of the goal, they are the ones who decide what to do next. There's no harm in setting a high goal for an important learning target.

Any SMART goal, by definition, contains five parts:

- **S**pecific—states the learning as clearly as possible;
- **M**easurable—can be assessed using CFA items that the team creates;
- **A**chievable—is able to be reached, based on current data and predictions;
- **R**elevant—aligns with long-term school improvement goals; and
- **T**ime-oriented—sets a timetable or deadline for achievement.

Here is an example of a correctly written SMART goal:

The percentage of fifth-grade students proficient and higher in writing a summary paragraph based on the reading of a short informational text will increase from 39 to 50 percent as measured by a short constructed-response item on the unit test, which will be administered on September 10 or 11.

Here is an example of an incorrectly stated SMART goal:

Fourth-grade students will improve in long division as measured by a chapter test.

The timeliness of the goal is critical. Teams must set short-cycle goals so that they can monitor students' progress incrementally and make adjustments to instruction as needed. The most effective Data Teams set goals that are to be achieved in two to six weeks, and they change their strategies throughout that time frame depending on how well or how poorly things are going.

It is also important not to establish the goal based on incomplete information or emotions. In working with several teams that are adamant students cannot write complete sentences, when data is collected on just that skill, it shows that almost all students can indeed write complete sentences. We have also worked with teams that allow themselves to be persuaded to set goals about things that only one or two teachers feel strongly about or that are only tangentially related to the prioritized standard being tracked. One notable example recalled is a team that wanted all students to be able to solve analogies. Another is a team that wanted to monitor how well students could demonstrate MLA formatting in their papers.

Lastly, remember not to get sidetracked by outliers—those particular questions or answers on an assessment that are wildly different from most others. For example, if there is one poorly worded question on an assessment, and the team did not catch the problem before the assessment was administered, almost all students could have answered it incorrectly. While this situation is interesting, it is not worthy of lengthy discussion in the Data Team meeting. The item could be disregarded entirely in the calculation of proficiency rates to diminish its impact, and the meeting could proceed. However, when team members spend too much time analyzing a flawed item, they steal precious time from analyzing other aspects of student work that could be far more illustrative.

Effective teams consistently craft SMART goals that guide their work. Whether or not they meet their goal in any given instructional cycle is less important than what they do in response to the results. They do not get discouraged when they fall short of a goal but immediately make plans for what they should do next to meet it or surpass it.

Step Four: Select Instructional Strategies

Step four is where the magic happens. It should constitute the bulk of the meeting, and it should be focused on looking forward, not backward. In this step, teachers must consider how they taught the concepts and skills, but more importantly, they must look forward with an eye toward innovation. The goal is to teach toward the desired learning targets in fresh, new ways. Step four is very much about the adage "if we do things the same way we've been doing them, we'll get the same results we got before."

Data Team members must consider the prioritized learning needs from step two as they determine the actions they will take. To be highly fruitful, they must discuss specific, research-based instructional strategies that they feel will have immediate impact on student learning.

Instructional strategies are the actions of the teacher that increase cognition in relation to an identified learning goal. Strategies are not activities like "Practice with ratios and proportions." That statement is not a strategy because it tells what the student will do, not what the teacher will do. Strategies are also not agenda items or class activities like a bell ringer or exit ticket (although teachers can certainly enact certain strategies during such activities). Strategies are written from the point of view of the adults who will be responsible for using them. They should be as specific as possible; for example, "Use the jigsaw method to teach the concepts of the separation of powers in government" and "Use a comparison matrix graphic organizer for note-taking so that students can readily see the similarities and differences among the indigenous groups studied in the unit."

Some teams may have a limited knowledge of research-based strategies. Some teams may focus on activities instead of strategies. Some teams focus on strategies about the learning environment rather than about instruction. Examples of these include allowing flexible seating, creating word walls, setting up classroom libraries, and posting anchor charts on the walls. While these things are certainly helpful to students, they are not actions directly aligned with urgent needs in most cases, and they are not adult actions. Materials are also not strategies. Packets or other items purchased from online, for-profit sites are not strategies; they are materials (and questionable ones at that).

Some teams discuss strategies that are only loosely related to the learning goals. For example, if the learning target (and SMART goal) indicates that students will be proficient in solving two-step equations, the strategy of asking students to set personalized goals would not be as effective as having them use a mnemonic device that helps them remember the order of steps to take when faced with such a problem.

Effective teams analyze each idea offered in terms of impact on student learning. They are able to tightly "fit" research-based strategies to student needs and spend time discussing how the strategies can be carried out with fidelity. This means that they take time to discuss how each of them will enact the strategy, including the teachers' specific actions and the time spent on those actions. They also discuss what resources they'll need, and some teams we've observed also talk about how they'll support each other.

There should be explicit evidence of each person's use of the agreed-upon strategies. A teammate, instructional coach, or administrator should be able to visit the classrooms and tell what the teachers are doing differently from what they had done before. As the team refines and strengthens practices, they can be applied in the future more readily. They can also be replicated throughout a building or an entire school system.

Exemplary teams choose strategies that have broad impact—across subjects, across grade levels, and in many areas of a student's academic life. Being able to write an accurate summary or being able to use a certain graphic organizer to represent what was learned are two examples of broad impact strategies.

Exemplary teams also study effective strategies with each other, during team meetings as time allows, and outside of team meetings as part of their own professional growth. They ensure every team member knows how to implement the agreed-upon strategies, teaching each other as necessary. These teams are also often called upon by administrators to share their successful practices with other teachers so that replication occurs. One of the best benefits of Data Team work is that highly successful strategies ripple throughout a building like water ripples in a pond when a pebble is tossed in.

Step Five: Determine Results Indicators

The final step in a Data Team meeting is determining results indicators, which may be both quantitative and qualitative. This step helps teachers to monitor progress toward the SMART goal and to gauge the success of the instructional strategies.

At their core, results indicators are if-then statements. In short, *if* teachers implement this strategy, *then* students and teachers see these results indicators. Results indicators are critical to monitor the adult actions that have caused changes in student learning.

Results indicators delineate adult actions and behaviors, student actions and behaviors, and evidence that the implemented strategies are having the desired results. They are important "look-fors" that let the team know their instructional strategies are working. They can also provide coaches and administrators with specifics that help them support the team members.

One Data Team in New York worked over a period of several months on summarizing and note-taking with their middle school students. As they implemented several strategies, these are some of the results indicators they listed:

- Students display conceptual knowledge of summarizing when participating in class discussions, using words such as *concise* and *delete*.
- Teachers of all subjects require students to write one summary paragraph per week, focused on the content of the class. These summary paragraphs are increasingly becoming more focused and cohesive.
- In science classes, students are becoming increasingly adept at writing the summary portion of Cornell notes.

Data Teams that are not yet adept at results indicators may simply state expected student achievement results. They may say something like, "Most students will be able to produce an effective summary paragraph when asked to do so." While this is a results indicator, it is not as specific and clear as the examples above.

Some teams also struggle with describing the explicit teacher actions that indicate the teacher is implementing the agreed-upon instructional strategies with fidelity. They may say a results indicator is, "The graphic organizer that the team agreed on is posted on each teacher's wall." A better results indicator statement would be, "Each teacher models the use of the graphic organizer two or three times weekly during writing workshop time." The best results indicators are highly specific and link directly to an action, whether it is the adult action that led to a change in learning or the student action that proves increased proficiency. To continue with the example about summarizing, a student-oriented results indicator might be, "Students are observed using the graphic organizer they were taught not only during the language arts class but also during social studies and science instruction without being prompted by the teacher."

A results indicator more rooted in student work might be, "Students start their summaries with topic sentences that are focused on the most important features of the information."

The most successful teams go above and beyond by establishing interim check-in times to monitor implementation of the strategies, rather than waiting for the next meeting. These teams also write clear, detailed descriptions of their results indicators so that other teachers can replicate the strategies.

Results indicators help team members predict student performance on the next formative assessment, and ultimately, on the summative assessment. It is important to craft them with care so that the teachers can clearly tie their actions to student performance. Ankhe Bradley and Tricia Nagel highlight this point.

INSIGHTS FROM COLLEAGUES

Ankhe Bradley, assistant superintendent, and Tricia Nagel, director of instruction, Joliet Schools, Joliet, Illinois

The Data Teams process is the heart of our organization. This process allows for Joliet to provide a common set of expectations, a framework, and language. The steps of the Data Team cycle are designed to support teams in diving deep in data analysis and promote a system of collective efficacy. One of the factors that has been most important to us is that it places students at the center of the discussion and provides a variety of opportunities for educators to share best practices in a collaborative environment. The Data Teams process allows teachers to set a common goal and analyze student data at the grade, school, and district level. Teams are able to analyze student work and identify misconceptions and reteach opportunities. Teams are in the driver's seat when it comes to goal setting and can collect a variety of student data to include extended responses, common assessments, essays, music checklists, and artwork rubrics. The Data Team process allows our teams to celebrate student success and pivot when the data suggests gaps in learning.

Richard DuFour (2010) said that collaborative teams are the fundamental building blocks of any learning organization and that they are "the best structure for achieving challenging goals" (p. 15). Data Teams are a vehicle that marries collaboration with classroom-based action research. When teachers are part of these continuously learning teams, the sky is the limit.

QUESTIONS TO CONSIDER

1. How are the meetings my team currently has similar to what is described in this chapter? How are they different from what is described?
2. What ideas in this chapter would I like to discuss with my team?
3. How can I help my team move forward?

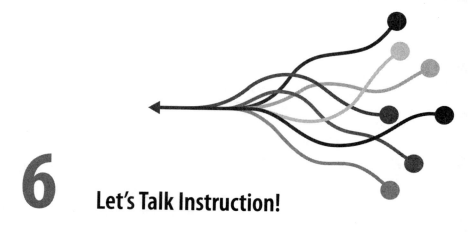

6 Let's Talk Instruction!

*Average teachers teach a skill until students get it right; highly effective
teachers work with students until they can't get it wrong.*
—Eric Jensen, *Engaging Students with Poverty in Mind*

Talk of learning and instruction often gets the largest amount of time in
team meetings. Why? The most common responses fit into three buckets:
trying to be efficient in the face of time pressures; thinking that curriculum
guides will cover what is necessary; and limiting talk to which activities or
products the students need to engage in or produce. Author and consultant Karen Power (2020) has expressed what so many teachers experience:
that as the dust settles in the first few weeks of September, conversations
about student learning deepen. Through collaboration, teachers and leaders use evidence to ensure that they understand the learning gaps students
have returned to school with and are working diligently to meet them
where they are, moving learning forward and at the same time, providing
interventions as support. Karen shares in her blog, "Sounds like quite a
balancing act, right? Yes, it is and it is what teachers do!"

Nearly everything in schools now occurs at warp speed. System-wide
pacing guides often count on students understanding enough about the
content in a day or two. There is a real sense that teaching has taken "tyranny of the urgent" as the typical frame for teachers' work. "What" has to
be done becomes the central focus instead of how students are learning
and mastering the content bit by bit. The three buckets (time constraints,
the curriculum guide will cover it, and talking about learning) take longer than just choosing an activity to do. However, as teachers use team
meeting time effectively, the discussions around learning and instruction
become the sweet spot of the work. If you leave a Data Team meeting and

haven't discussed how instruction will change, then you haven't really had a Data Team meeting. As Paul Bambrick-Santoyo points out in *Driven by Data 2.0*, 2019, p. 5), "To teach our students what they need to be successful, we need to clearly define what they must learn and be able to do; set clear progress points they'll need to meet along the way; and keep an eye on other signs that show whether they're learning so we can course-correct sooner rather than later if they aren't."

Curriculum guides spell out how to teach concepts so that teachers narrow their learning strategies to those presented in the guide. That works for many students but misses others. If a formative assessment indicates that students are struggling, a teacher's default is often reteaching. Thus, the teacher returns to the same system and methods just with a new-looking paper and pencil route or saying it again a little slower and sometimes even a bit louder. Slower and louder are not innovative teaching strategies.

Professional learning communities often focus more attention on student activities and work products rather than on the learning process, even though the word *learning* is part of the name. Of course, the team is concerned about as many students as possible reaching proficiency or mastery—and yet, our instructional practices work best when we learn to see the thinking and learning through the eyes of students. Read what happens when science teacher Randy Hardigree started seeing his work through new eyes.

INSIGHTS FROM COLLEAGUES

Randy Hardigree, biology teacher, LaGrange High school, LaGrange, Georgia.

I was asked what has changed for me? I will attempt to encapsulate it.
- I build opportunities into each day to organically stimulate students to think—even if it sometimes takes us out of the content area. I had to give myself permission to do that. This takes time, and making it work involves choosing effective prompts that are interesting, challenging, relevant, personal, and even emotional. Good prompts level the playing field. I'm always on a quest to find things that students have no frame of reference for. This raises participation, because nobody has the advantage.

(Continued)

- My language is different. I make my own wonderings and curiosities apparent by thinking out loud. I follow questions with others like "What makes you say that?" and "What are you wondering about this?" and "What did you notice?" We talk about the difference between knowledge and understanding.
- We live by these daily goals: Did you *think for yourself*? Did you *share out* your thoughts with others? Did you *listen* to the thoughts of others? If these three things haven't happened, the day is not complete. My students spend the year in community groups of four—the makeup of the four people often changing. This establishes a necessary level of mutual trust. Operating within this familiar thinking cluster helps students meet their three daily goals. What a joy to see the "invisible" students find their own voices and to see the "Pick me! Pick me!" students find joy in listening to the thoughts of their classmates!
- Learning is now seen, thought of, and talked about as a continuum. All assessments are formative until they're not. That sounds odd, but I'm so far removed from grades. I have to use grades because I'm required to report them. But I've worked so hard to help students become aware of their own places on the learning continuum. What did they understand *before*? Where are they *now*? What needs to happen to reach the goal of *understanding*? What am I *curious* about now that I understand? Assessments identify where we are at this point in time and inform us about what needs to happen next. We're all at different places on that continuum, but we will all reach that target of mastery.
- I have far to go, but the culture of my classroom is different to the core. I am no longer the dispenser of knowledge. I'm a participant in the learning just as much as my students are. Thinking happens here, and thinking gets deep. I know from student feedback that they feel comfortable, safe, confident, interested, challenged, and happy in my classroom each day. And it's really no surprise that my state test scores are perfectly fine!

This teacher's eyes now light up when he talks about student learning! That is what teaching and learning can be. John Hattie (2017) states, "A good teacher has high expectations, creates an error-friendly climate in the classroom, constantly questions his or her actions and impact, continuously evaluates his or her own teaching and works together with other teachers to understand what they mean by impact and to evaluate this impact. Good teachers impact on all students' learning" (p. 5). Isn't that what we want, to have an impact? This is the why that led many of us to the field and that keeps us here.

It requires finding the right balance of rigor and relevance.

Degrees of Rigor and Relevance

ICLE lays out four quadrants of learning (see Figure 6.1). Bernadette Lambert (2016) in *Moving Beyond Quadrant A* discusses the overlay of the Application Model on the Knowledge Taxonomy yielding four quadrants. Each quadrant reveals the degree to which both rigor and relevance are utilized. John Hattie (2012) asserts from his research that up to 90 percent

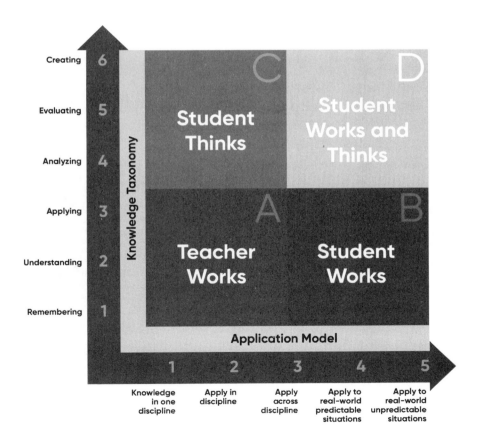

FIGURE 6.1   Teacher and Student Roles in Rigorous Learning

of the instruction we conduct can be completed by students using only the surface-level skills. That would have us staying in Quadrant A.

The model provides a resource for assessing where we are as we look at the evidence of student learning to date. The model also provides a common language to help in identifying mistakes and planning next steps—all to deepen student learning.

Now let's review what the quadrants actually include. It is important to notice that each quadrant (Figure 6.2) has its own important purpose related to the content and skills in any standard.

• Quadrant A: Students gather and store bits of knowledge and information and are primarily expected to understand and remember this knowledge.

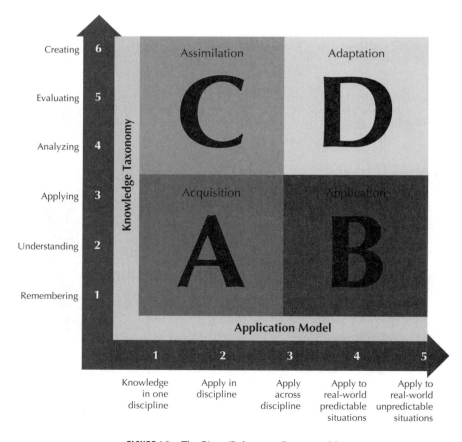

FIGURE 6.2   The Rigor/Relevance Framework®

- Quadrant B: Students use acquired knowledge to solve problems, design solutions, and complete work.
- Quadrant C: Students extend and refine their acquired knowledge so they can draw upon this knowledge automatically and use it to routinely solve problems.
- Quadrant D: Students have the competence to think in complex ways and apply their knowledge and skills even when confronted with unusual or perplexing unknowns.

The quadrant model is actually in sync with what modern brain research has shown. Instruction must take into consideration the following: how the brain functions in learning; receiving and paying attention; deliberately using the working memory; and practicing until knowledge is moved to storage in the long-term memory. Students make their learning their own in this process. They then use the concepts to be innovative and able to think with complexity about how concepts can be combined, demonstrating their mastery of the standards that cause them to be proficient and go beyond. To move a student along this path, you need to:

- State a clear direction for learning.
- Conduct a brain-friendly lesson introduction that draws in the senses with the power to incorporate previous knowledge and experience to apply to the work at hand.
- Invite students to engage. Remember that we can draw learners in with attention, but we can only invite engagement. The two often get conflated into one. That engagement allows the learner to persevere to work through deliberate practice, and then encodes the information to the long-term memory. That is when the power of cognition really takes over.
- Orchestrate an independent task that calls on recall and thinking to build, create, and combine that knowledge in new ways that make learning the learner's own.

The Toolkit that you'll find online (www.leadered.com/plc-datateams) and excerpted in the Appendix will give you multiple ways to create successful thinking and learning for your students. The resources there will support good questions, effective technology use, and engagement strategies. You can use the Toolkit to select specific approaches to meet each student's need. Many teachers treat these strategies almost like a recipe card: do these actions in this order and it will work.

Then comes the challenge of translating the strategies into collaborative opportunities.

Essential Learning Requires Collaboration

Using collaboration (or "co-laboring") allows students to do what is so essential to learning—socialize to test, articulate, and expand their own thoughts. The more teachers learn about the work of collaboration, the more they can bring it back to students. Used effectively, collaborative work takes students consistently to Quadrant C and Quadrant D with real frequency. Kathryn Girard describes how this works.

INSIGHTS FROM COLLEAGUES

Kathryn Girard, elementary teacher, East Gresham Elementary, Gresham, Oregon

Collaboration is an essential part of the learning process for teachers, it is where we get to build on our knowledge by absorbing others'. Why can't it be for students also?

I introduced ways for my students to collaborate through different turn-and-talk strategies. That simple change had a profound impact on my students' learning. As they got more comfortable with the structure of collaboration, I looked for more ways to implement it—Socratic seminars, jigsaws, brainstorm carousels, post-test review. With each new strategy I saw engagement and learning increase. By allowing my students multiple opportunities throughout the day to collaborate, I gave them a way to learn more from each other than they ever would from just me. I gave them an additional teacher in the form of their peers.

Kathryn's collaboration with her colleagues brought her confidence, enthusiasm, joy of learning, and skills back to her classroom. Her students benefited. All learning is social, after all. As soon as you have discovered something new, what is your first response—to tell someone! In *Breaking Bold*, Weston and Molly Kieschnick (2020) remind teachers of three central reasons to have students doing collaborative work:

- Interpersonal joy leads to peak experiences;
- Through collaboration, students must make use of and practice a range of social and emotional skills; and
- Creating some sort of innovative work product is real-world relevant.

Learning and thinking moving to mastery is the "why" we do this work. Teachers want their students to learn and learn deeply. This is what all of the previous chapters have been building. Instruction is what drives that success. Our advice to teachers is to think beyond the tyranny of the urgent tasks of being in the classroom, pacing guides, and curriculum guides. Instead, work collaboratively with the excitement of how it feels when we are part of successful student learning! When more students than ever master what you want them to master, this is what you as a "lead learner" in the classroom want. This is how teachers see their teaching through their students' eyes and how students see their teachers as learners. Can you think of anything better than that?

QUESTIONS TO CONSIDER

1. What have I learned lately that took me through the steps talked about in this chapter?
2. When did I see my students thinking and learning as described in this chapter?
3. What three words would I use to describe my teaching at its best?
4. What change could I make to create instructional practices that helps students learn?

7

How Do We Start, Provide Accountability, and Sustain This Work?

Always plan for the fact that no plan ever goes according to plan.
—Simon Sinek, *Together Is Better*

Educators should view starts, restarts, and redos through the Sinek model of the "why" of their work. Kyra Donovan (Ainsworth and Donovan, 2019) demonstrates this in *Rigorous Curriculum Design* when she talks about starting work in a new district. In Kyra's experience introducing curriculum design to educators and school leaders, she found it critical to focus first on the why (the purpose of the work) and its benefits to students with clear learning outcomes. She also focused on how to achieve those learning outcomes and how they benefit teachers by providing clarity and focus on what to teach, when to teach it all, and how to assess student achievement.

This chapter is different from the others in this book. It is a veritable buffet of Insights from Colleagues. We wanted you to hear from people doing the work because the work needs to be customized to fit your system, school, or team. Our suggestion is that you take note of new ideas and consider a tweak of current practices if an insight provides a catalyst for further dialogue.

We have discussed why we do this work, how to set it up, and the importance of keeping learning and instruction at the center. Where are you in this journey? There are still school systems that are either starting teams for the first time or restarting after finding that previous starts couldn't be sustained. Why does that happen? This chapter may help you determine what might have been missing or what can make your work have more impact. Let's first look at starting the work from different perspectives.

Starting or Restarting

In their book *The Transformative Power of Collaborative Inquiry*, Donohoo and Velasco (2016) make clear that "while collaborative inquiry has the potential to transform school improvement, simply putting structures in place for teams to come together and inquire about their practice is not enough to realize the transformation. Giving teachers time and resources to collaborate does not mean that they have the knowledge and desire to meaningfully do so" (p. 15).

A long-term plan is central to the success for a whole school system. This is articulated so clearly by Ankhe Bradley.

INSIGHTS FROM COLLEAGUES

Ankhe Bradley, assistant superintendent, Joliet Schools, Joliet, Illinois

The Data Teams process has transformed the way Joliet Public Schools District #86 approaches the cycle of continuous improvement. Our journey began by designing a five-year plan to ensure that we were thoughtful about planning intentional professional learning for administrators, classroom teachers, and instructional coaches. In the beginning we focused on the core components of the Data Team process, allocating time for collaboration, and building trusting relationships with grade-level teams. The next phase included providing staff "sandbox" time to select a goal and practice completing a Data Team learning cycle. This allowed time for teams to provide feedback on the process, select reporting documents, and most importantly, it provided teams the opportunity to feel success with accomplishing grade-level learning goals. Currently, we are in the monitoring phase where each grade-level team presents to the entire staff at the end of each trimester. These grade-level presentations provide an opportunity for staff to celebrate, ask clarifying questions, provide recommendations, and discuss the next steps in the learning process. We are proud that the Data Team process has become the Joliet way of deepening our learning about quality instructional practices, standards-based instruction, quality assessment, student work, and meaningful feedback with students and families.

Ankhe Bradley presented their thoughtful and intentional five-year plan. This planning is central to the success of the work. A cultural assessment and shift are great first steps. If we were to walk the halls of your school today, what would we see and hear?

- How many conversations would you hear about learning?
  - Teacher to teacher
  - Teacher to student
  - Student to student
  - Instructional leader to student
- How many conversations would you hear about how far you are and where you still need to go to achieve mastery of a given standard?
- How many students are talking about their own evidence of progress?
- How many celebratory conversations of new levels of learning would you hear?
- How many conversations of teachers quickly sharing with each other what is working or what needs a tweak?

Adam Drummond (2019) is the author of *The Instructional Change Agent.* He shares with us what he remembers of his principalship and describes his experience about building a "Community of Excellence."

INSIGHTS FROM COLLEAGUES

Adam Drummond, associate partner at ICLE

When I was hired to be the principal of Lincoln Elementary, it was made clear that there needed to be immediate improvement in academic performance. The question was "How do you do that?" There are literally thousands of variables that impact the positive or negative performance and growth of students, so how do you know where to start? Over a five-year period, we were able to increase English/language arts scores by 13.1 percent and math scores by 12.4 percent. As I reflect back on how this attainment occurred, three main strategies were employed.

1. *Move Together:* One of the first actions was to get input from the staff on what was working and what wasn't working. We then developed

a plan of action that included a unified mission and vision that everyone knew. A "Community of Excellence" became our marching orders for students and staff alike. We used this vision as the filter for all decision making.

2. *Pre- and Post-assessment:* We developed a pre- and post-assessment process for instruction. We had a yearlong calendar that showed which priority standards we were going to pre-assess, teach, and post-assess. Each standard(s)—never more than two at the same time—was mapped into two- to three-week increments with error analysis conducted to determine the root cause of mislearning. This was time intensive, but powerful in moving the needle. Weekly Data Team meetings were held to discuss the performance, error analysis, and instructional methods for mastery learning.

3. *Reimagining the School Day:* To build toward mastery learning, we needed a master schedule that allowed the opportunity for actual mastery of learning to occur. We developed an "Eagle Time" and a "Success Time" for ELA and math, specifically. Each grade level had its own 30 to 60 minutes in reading for differentiation and small group; this was separate from the state-mandated 90-minute reading block. Students were flexed into this time, and all available staff had small groups. For math, we had a K–2 time and a grades 3–5 time. All students were again grouped based on pre-test scores. Some students were moved into groups outside their grade level to help support their learning for remediation and acceleration. In other words, instruction was data-driven and personalized based on student mastery.

I am sure there were many other ways we invested in building a "Community of Excellence." What I know is that it took 100 percent of the staff invested in making a difference in the lives of our students. We all rolled up our sleeves (I even taught 30 minutes of math instruction in our Success Time) to make sure every student had their needs met. These strategies aren't overly complicated. Why they worked was the commitment that was made to ensure success.

There is no minimizing how important it is to create a culture that reflects learning, excellence, and each student's ability to achieve. That kind of culture is central to doing this kind of collaborative work. We can see this from Theresa Rouse's perspective as a new superintendent.

INSIGHTS FROM COLLEAGUES

Theresa Rouse, superintendent, Joliet Schools, Joliet, Illinois

As a new superintendent, there is a window of time within the review of current systems and recommendations for change to happen. Professional learning communities and focused approaches toward how student data is embraced can make or break the progress needed in a school district. Professional time during the work day ensures a higher degree of accountability for professional learning communities to function well. Time was the missing logistical element we needed to shift our focus to intentional processes to address our student data to impact meaningful change.

To provide the time needed, we instituted a new model of delivery of music and art for elementary-age students. We hired certified music and art teachers who began to provide a 90-minute block once every nine days. This allowed grade-level teachers at elementary schools to meet for a dedicated 90 minutes during the professional work day. In our second year of implementation, we were able to hire additional certified music and art teachers, which allowed us to provide the 90-minute block once every seven days.

The next step in ensuring high-quality professional learning community time happened was to train our leadership on the Data Team process. Leadership trained the building leadership teams for implementation at the grade level. Instructional coaches were trained to provide another layer of support at the classroom teacher level in the grade-level meetings.

A district-level Data Team was created to establish forms and processes for consistent implementation across the 20 school sites in the district. The district team consists of site- and district-level administrators, as well as instructional coaches. This team continues to meet to refine the Data Teams' forms and processes based on the feedback from teachers as they work through implementation.

Professional coaching for site administrators has allowed us to further deepen and embed the Data Teams process into all aspects of the implementation of Data Teams in our professional learning community setting. This includes how we set goals, how we analyze formative and summative data, and how we make decisions about what is needed for individual students.

At the end of each trimester, grade levels are responsible to present to their colleagues a Data Team task that reflects their grade-level student data and how the team is implementing the process established by the district team. All presentations are shared across the district for the purpose of taking the mystery out of student achievement data. To facilitate the sharing of promising practices across the district, the district Data Team and the building leadership teams gather once each year.

We consider ourselves a work in progress as we continue to refine and adjust the Data Teams process for our district implementation. As more and more of our education professionals embrace and embed the transparency of student achievement data into their day-to-day engagement with students, the gains will be obvious in our individual and overall results.

The Data Teams process has provided us a common language and approach to how we analyze, discuss, plan, and reflect on both formative and summative data. The impacts and effects of the work we have done thus far will be visible as we continue to embed the process in everything we do!

The common language and approach are central to having successful implementation. What if you were a teacher turned principal in your first assignment? Linda Bishop had a front-row seat.

INSIGHTS FROM COLLEAGUES

Linda Bishop, instructional and leadership coach, University of Oregon

Data Teams, or PLCs, have been around for a decade or more with slight variations, and teachers and administrators are familiar with the theory behind them. Many schools say, "We do Data Teams." Data Team training has been performed in countless school districts for thousands of teachers. However, in many schools Data Teams are not effective in improving student outcomes. Why is this, and what can we do about it?

Whether you set out to establish Data Teams with a staff who has never done them, or you need to refresh a staff who has drifted away from their intent, careful consideration is needed in several areas for the initiative to be successful. Teachers need concrete models and supports in the initial stages, helping them build a framework for the collaborative work to come. We found that teachers understood the idea of Data Teams but might be unclear or need practice in some phases of the process. The following suggestions came from my work as a leadership coach with Todd, an elementary principal, who was leading his staff to Data Teams for the first time. They take time to establish, but it is worth it.

- Todd created a master schedule that allowed each grade level to have common prep time at least a couple of times per week and carved out an additional 25-minute slot, dedicated to Data Teams. He met with each team during this time weekly.
- Their district had a 75-minute late opening on Wednesday mornings twice a month, dedicated to Data Teams. All grade-level teams met in the library during this time. The principal, coach, and specialists could easily move between teams, supporting their efforts.
- As a pilot project, we created an artificial four-week cycle framework that clearly directed teachers' actions for each week, helping them understand what to do and when. The calendar was published and referred to weekly in the principal's newsletter to staff. We ran this four-week cycle for two months using a common content—math—as an easy first step.
  - Week 1: Pretest / Collect and Chart Data / Instruction / Instruction / Instruction
  - Week 2: Instruction / Formative Assessments / Instruction / Instruction
  - Week 3: Instruction / Formative Assessments / POSTTEST late this week
  - Week 4: Instruction / RETEACH WEEK / PRETEST for next standard late in week

- Todd created a simple common Data Team form for all to use. It was predictable and supported the cycle. Teams used the same form for the entire four-weeks of the cycle, filling it in electronically as they progressed through the process. This form changed over time; however, the school still uses a common form.
- Leadership is key in the effort to make Data Teams effective. Leaders need to be consistently present, listening for areas of need in furthering professional development and support. Areas such as building trust, increasing rigor, formative assessments, data literacy, higher order questioning, feedback, brain research, using effective instructional strategies, progress monitoring, differentiating instruction, and many other topics may need to be revisited.

After initially practicing the steps, teams adjusted the timing of the cycle and jumped into real Data Teams. Given support, teacher teams can build on a Data Team framework that will lead to deepening their use of effective professional practices and effect positive changes for students.

Clearly Todd and Linda were deliberate and detailed about their work with the whole staff. The collaborative structure needs to be planned with intentionality. So, once that is done, how is a system successfully implemented and sustained? Again, there must be a plan. There must be a measure of accountability, too.

Accountability

Accountability can make the difference between another initiative started and lost or a long-term piece of a system's culture. One way to support Data Team work is to go back to the four ICLE quadrants (Figure 7.1) and know what to look for in the functioning of the team and their meetings. In the work with Joliet Public Schools District #86, the basic concepts from the quadrants (Chapter 6) were adapted to look at that support giving formative feedback through visits to the PLC.

C Emerging	D Excelling
• Data/evidence collected • Data/evidence discussed • Teams use documentation • SMART goal set • Result indicators possibilities discussed • Team identifies connections between	• Data/evidence recorded and reviewed before meeting • Student work compared/used in the meeting • Data/evidence analyzed for common misconceptions • Teams create documentation that works for the team • SMART goal set efficiently • Instructional practices designed that move all students forward • Frequent formative assessments • Result indicators are coupled with instructional practices and identifiable in the classroom • Celebration for students and adults is frequent
A Ready to Grow	B Growing
• Teams meet at appointed times • Document forms are present • Five steps are identified • Need for evidence is identified • SMART goal discussed • Unit/lesson plans discussed • Academic achievement appears minimal	• Data/evidence submitted before meeting • Data/evidence discussed • Teams use documentation • SMART goal set • Possible strategies chosen • Result indicators possibilities discussed

FIGURE 7.1   Quadrants in Developing Data Teams

Looking at Teams Through the Quadrants

The quadrant template is meant to allow for feedback and build trust that all are in this together. If the accountability is only mandated, then the whole effort can spiral into one more program of compliance. If, on the other hand, the changes are built on mutual commitments evident in actions between administration and teachers, then there is evidence that leads to collective trust. Kourtney Ferrua captures the idea of mutual commitment as she reflects on her position of principal.

INSIGHT FROM COLLEAGUES

Kourtney Ferrua, director of curriculum, instruction and assessment, McMinnville, Oregon

The Data Team process has been integral to the success in our district. When I served as principal at Wascher Elementary we were in the lowest quadrant of the state for student achievement, which absolutely did not reflect the work and dedication of our teaching staff. The problem was that we were all working hard, but independently. It's hard to move a ship when you are not synchronized. To make the change, we doubled down on the Data Team process. With Rigorous Curriculum Design, we aligned standards and assessments and tripled the number of Data Team meetings we had. This meant three Data Team meetings a month and only one faculty meeting. The truth is that without outcomes for students, you can "professional development" your staff to death, but not change a thing for students. We wanted to focus and change the trajectory for our students. We all met in the library at the same time, and for the first few months we did the process in a guided way. We gave more time to the steps that gave the biggest bang for our buck, analyzed student evidence, and determined instructional strategies and adult actions. As we got better at the process, the meeting took about 45 minutes. Given that we had an hour together, I started to add back in professional development for the first 15 minutes. It felt like a commercial for an instructional strategy, a summary of a research article, or a dialogue about an education blog. The uniting thread was that the professional development could be implemented immediately in their Data Team process. If we had just had a 15-minute reminder on the impact of feedback, the challenge that day might be to consider how feedback could impact student achievement in their Data Team meeting. Within a few months, the boat started to gain some momentum. It was palpable in our meetings. No longer were the conversations going to things outside of our control, but instead they were focused, relevant, and about student achievement. Within a year we went from the lowest quadrant to the top 10 percent in growth in our state. In 2018, we were the highest achieving Title I school in our state. The Data Team process is not a magic bullet that makes the work easier, it *is* the work. It provides the structure to invest focus and energy where it matters most for kids.

When a school finds the kind of success that Kourtney describes, there is no stopping them. The same is true of a team finding success as we shared in Chapter 2—no stopping that team from wanting to do this work. Dr. Robert Culp shares his thoughts of how an effective team structures their work so that they want to keep replicating their success.

INSIGHTS FROM COLLEAGUES

Dr. Robert Culp, instructional coach, Joliet, Illinois

One of the most beneficial tasks we do as a Data Team is designing assessments together and determining the criteria for success. Successful Data Teams collaborate and go through a five-stage process:

1. Decide what data we want to attain and design the task/assessment.
2. Create a rubric collaboratively, ensuring it stays focused on the data we are collecting.
3. Several, if not all, team members complete the task/assessment to have examples.
4. The team grades the examples together to ensure all approach gathering data through the same lens.
5. Revise as needed.

This process of practicing "dogfooding," that is, using your own product before giving it to students, ensures Data Team conversations are focused and significant. Once we started utilizing this practice, our Data Teams found that the rubrics and assignments were often not gathering the data we thought they were, or were not quite as clear, focused, and universal as we had thought.

Now that we have implemented this as our norm, our Data Team meetings are more productive, focused, and truly assist in improving student achievement.

The accountability that Robert described was based on support and collaboration in the work that needed to be done. It was not found in a mandate or on a checklist. How do we incorporate the culture of collaboration, dependence on evidence for decision making, and student learning and achievement in our classrooms, schools, and systems? The outcome leads to answers in how the work can be sustained.

Sustaining the Work

Sustainability requires candid conversations with leadership teams at the system, building, and team levels. Chapter 2 was about building teams before having conversations about the question "What will accountability look like for us?" Having a working definition of *accountability* makes all the difference in uniting not only what you're doing and how you're doing it, but also why you are committed to this work. Part of being the instructional leader in the building or at the system level is initiating these important conversations.

Another way to have a principal provide mutual accountability and sustainability is with one-on-one "growth conversations" beyond the team meetings. Principal Vernicia Gee-Davis did the work with her people.

INSIGHT FROM COLLEAGUES

Vernicia Gee-Davis, principal, Pershing Elementary, Joliet, Illinois

Student growth has been sustained through individual teacher data meetings, which are held every four to five weeks. These meetings are created as a follow up to grade-level meetings. I'm able to meet with teachers about the strengths and opportunities of their specific classrooms and specific students. We have goal systems in place at every level (school-wide, grade level, classroom, students) to create a culture of growth. The data conversations are all about student growth. We create standards-based goals from multiple data sets. Growth conversations between teachers and students after benchmark and progress monitoring is key. Students are aware of their progress, which allows them to take ownership of learning progress and growth. Students chart their growth and look forward to having conversations with their teachers. Students visit me to show their growth. Individual teacher data meetings allow us to be targeted around student growth, assessing needs, and adjusting instruction based upon reflection. We've had tremendous success and were recognized by our district because of it.

Gee-Davis illustrates the impact of growth conversations among all of the learning partners. She models having the conversations with teachers and they, in turn, have similar conversations with their students. She demonstrates what Michael Fullan calls a nuanced leader in his chapter on change agents in *10 Mindframes for Leaders* (Hattie and Smith, 2021). He states, "Nuanced leaders see details below the surface, while also seeing the big picture. They participate as learners; they can be experts on some things and apprentices on others" (p. 49). The questions and conversations can be key to sustaining the work of PLCs and Data Teams.

What Does Sustainability Look Like at the School Level?

How does one keep sustainability energized? Every school we have worked with wants to know how to do this. Many schools have come up with ways to do this, and we now get an opportunity to learn about them.

A trimester challenge is used by one district: each PLC comes to a faculty meeting talking about something that their team is learning either from success or challenge. Sitting in on those meetings and hearing teams dialogue and share with each other has been an excellent experience. Dr. Tricia Nagel describes those Trimester Data Challenges.

INSIGHTS FROM COLLEAGUES

Dr. Tricia Nagel, director of teaching and learning, Joliet, Illinois

Every trimester each PLC team "reports out" and shares their experiences in the Data Team process to the rest of their school colleagues during a School Improvement Day. A template is given to each team to review the steps of the Data Team process. This allows each team to reflect on the data and ask deeper questions of themselves as they create the presentation. We call this trimester reporting the Trimester Data Challenge. Along with reflection, we also emphasize sharing instructional strategies. This can be very rewarding to share strategies that, backed with data, make a difference in the growth of students. It is exciting to see data growth that another PLC wants to replicate and implement with a group of students. It is also rewarding to see teachers reflect on what can be done in the next data cycle to improve.

Ultimately, sustainability comes from teachers seeing the work pay off for their students. Whether on an individual or team level, people repeat behaviors that work. As you have read in previous chapters, if the team and their students have been successful, then there is no stopping both the celebration and the replication of what created that success.

While initiating the work and setting the structure of the PLC and Data Team work are crucial, some school systems forget that creating accountability and sustainability are crucial. In this chapter, multiple colleagues have shared how the work has kept the momentum moving forward. Just as in instruction, we don't want to simply stay in compliance or the first quadrant, in other words gathering information; rather, we want to gain deeper understanding that carries the work toward implementation. Together these actions transform learning for students.

QUESTIONS TO CONSIDER

1. What has kept PLCs and Data Teams working together at my school?
2. When have I enjoyed teamwork and what has made it enjoyable?
3. What would make the work more sustainable and fulfilling from my perspective? What do I want to try that I found in this chapter?

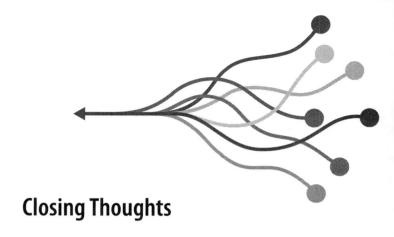

Closing Thoughts

May your choices reflect your hopes, not your fears.

—Nelson Mandela

From Polly

It all comes together for me in the billboard slogan mentioned back in Chapter 1: stronger me's make stronger we's. As each of us grow personally and professionally, we contribute to building a stronger team.

Am I learning and growing in my own efficacy? Have you known someone who has strong self-efficacy? As one keeps learning, others are drawn toward that person to listen and learn. I know I am working in my area of passion about learning when I lose track of time. This is what Mihaly Csikszentmihalyi, author of *Flow* and *Creativity*, calls flow. Are you in the flow zone and can't wait to have the next conversation about learning? That is what I want for each of us as educators and as team members.

Secondly, am I seeing the best in others? Effective collaboration is only possible when I (we) do the inviting to practice Clark's four stages of psychological safety from Chapter 2, including learning, contributing, and challenging. Are we authentically inviting people to think and learn with us?

Thomas Murray (2019) in *Personal and Authentic*, states, "Right now, your school's culture perfectly aligns with the mindset and actions of the adults in your building. If we want things to change, we must look inward before we look around us. We must move forward if we want the whole group to move forward" (p. 23). To which I say a resounding, YES!

Angela collaborated with me, and now we ask you to continue thinking and learning!

From Angela

I first learned about Data Teams when I was a member of one. Our team worked with eighth-grade students at a chronically low-performing middle school, and oh my, we were so proud of those youngsters and of ourselves when we saw dramatic changes in student learning!

I later had the opportunity to support Data Team–powered PLCs all over the country (and in a couple of other countries) as a consultant, working and learning alongside colleagues like Polly, learning from those colleagues every day—and learning from all the wonderful practitioners we were supporting.

Almost two decades later, as we finish this book, I stand in awe of the thousands of educators who use the Data Team process to impact the lives of students in so many positive ways. The "we" is indeed stronger than "me" when it comes to moving as many students as possible to high levels of achievement.

My hope is that you will find within these pages not only encouragement and affirmation, but also some practical ideas that will improve the work of your team. Start with yourself, start small, start however you wish—but just *start*.

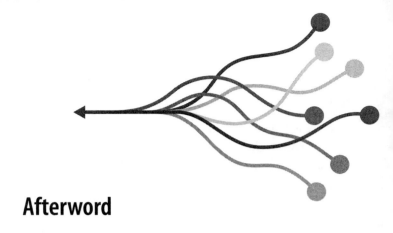

Afterword

As I write this, schools are continuing to face a litany of challenges in light of the double epidemic—the worldwide pandemic and the economic fallout that has impacted children, families, and schools. Underlying the current challenges that educators face is a divisive body-politic that has created a national climate where there have been incessant attacks and debates about science. More pointedly, there has been criticism about the utility of science and whether or not science matters. If so, whose science matters? What data are we to believe, and what data are we to dismiss?

The conundrum before us is that as educators try to plan for an uncertain future, a common phrase that has been used is "we will let the science inform our decision making." This powerful statement offers a sound and reasonable way to make critical decisions about how schools respond to changing learning needs, stronger calls for equity, and growing instances of emotional trauma. Moreover, there is also a need to acknowledge the tremendous amounts of stress and anxiety that teachers, staff, and school leaders experience during periods of transition and transformation.

Politics aside, there is a desperate need to rely on data, on sound empirically based evidence, to help us move forward if we are to reimagine schools. Even recently, schools are not working for many of our students. Moving forward, we know that technology offers some help, but not necessarily for every student or family. Millions of students never logged on during remote learning or could not be located—and schools are still at a loss to understand what happened to these students.[1] It will be vital for data collection efforts to inform a clear picture of the landscape of schools and to capture a snapshot of what school demographics look like over the next two years, five years, and even ten years. After recent disruptions, many students may never return, some may opt for hybrid approaches, and many will explore homeschooling as a solution. So, we need to understand who the students are that we are serving.

In addition, our data must help us understand the students who have suffered the most. Undoubtedly, over the years and through periods of disruption, our most vulnerable students have experienced even greater challenges. Thus, the need to have disaggregated data that will drill down to help us identify student populations that will require additional supports and interventions is essential. Many districts across the nation would recognize that students experiencing homelessness, those in foster care, those living in high poverty situations, and students who have special needs will require intense interventions. What many schools are less likely to discuss, though the data point this out, are the stubborn racial disparities that have only widened. Thus, data-informed conversations about race must be tackled head on. Now is not the time for avoidance, fear, uncertainty, or fragility when it comes to matters about racial equity.[2] Therefore, our data must be able to identify where we must be better when it comes to the needs of our BIPOC students and our multilingual students.

All of these concerns point to one simple fact: now is the time for professional learning communities (PLCs) to come together to reflect, think, strategize, and act with an explicit focus on data-driven decision making. In *PLC-Powered Data Teams*, Polly Patrick and Angela Peery provide educators with comprehensive guidance on how they can function as an effective team to gather and analyze evidence of work by students at the classroom level. Through their collaborative nature, PLCs can play an integral role in coming together to engage in dialogue, with data serving as an essential tool for (big and small) school transformation. What has worked for students during remote learning? We need to identify the bright spots that have been uncovered through direct experience. The importance of data is vital in both painting a clear picture of a school landscape and in supporting important conversations on equity, race, and access.

We must remember that data-driven discussions are necessary and can be uncomfortable because they can paint a disturbing picture about which students are being underserved. I recall being in a school district in Washington state where the superintendent centered an entire principal and leadership meeting around school discipline. To the surprise, and perhaps chagrin, of school leaders, the superintendent showed school-by-school data of suspensions broken down by race, gender, and incident type over a three-year window. The data revealed deeply troubling racial disparities that Black and Indigenous students faced. This experience then informed continuing discussions between educators at all levels throughout the district.

The data told a story. The data could not be refuted. School leaders had collected it, signed off on it, and sent it to district leaders. In closing, the superintendent challenged them to evaluate their data and to do better; to reduce suspensions, understand root causes, and let data-informed decision making guide the process.

This is how data can lead to difficult, yet necessary conversations. In this indispensable new edition of *PLC-Powered Data Teams*, Patrick and Peery offer all the necessary strategies to have similarly powerful conversations— and resulting initiatives—within every school. In this way, our BIPOC students, our multilingual students, and our striving students' experiences with learning can be transformed through the data teams process.

We need strong, reliable data sets. We need collaborative, team-based PLCs that collect, analyze, and use data to create more equitable schools equipped with transformative policies and practices that serve *all* students well.

In short, data matters. Let's use data to create the schools that our students deserve.

Tyrone C. Howard
University of California, Los Angeles

Notes

1. Kurtz, Holly. 2020. "In-Person Learning Expands, Student Absences Up, Teachers Work Longer, Survey Shows." Education Week, October 15, 2020. https://www.edweek.org/leadership/in-person-learning-expands-student-absences-up-teachers-work-longer-survey-shows/2020/10.
2. DiAngelo, Robin. 2018. *White Fragility: Why It's So Hard for White People to Talk About Racism.* New York: Random House.

APPENDIX

Excerpts from the Rigorous Learning Toolkit

To download the entire kit, please go to www.leadered.com/plc-datateams

Instructional Strategies and the Rigor/Relevance Framework

The strategies below are rated for their appropriateness to each quadrant.

Strategy	Quadrant A Acquisition	Quadrant B Application	Quadrant C Assimilation	Quadrant D Adaptation
Analogies	★★	★★	★★★	★★★
Analyzing video stimulus	★★	★★★	★★	★★
Brainstorming	★★	★	★★★	★★★
Compare and contrast	★★	★	★★★	★★
Cooperative learning	★★	★★★	★★	★★★
Crafting an argument	★★	★★	★★★	★★★
Demonstration	★	★★★	★	★★
Feedback and reflection	★★	★★	★★★	★★★
Guided practice	★★★	★★	★★	★
Inquiry	★	★★	★★	★★★
Learning centers	★★★	★★★	★★	★★
Lecture	★★★	★	★★	★
Manipulatives and models	★★★	★★★	★★★	★★
Memorization	★★★	★★	★★	★
Note-taking/graphic	★★	★★	★★	★★
Physical movement	★★	★★★	★★	★★
Pinwheel discussion	★★	★★	★★★	★★★
Problem-based learning	★★	★★★	★★	★★★
Semantic feature analysis	★★	★★	★★★	★★★
Simulation/role playing	★★	★★★	★★	★★★
Socratic seminar	★	★	★★★	★★★
Storytelling	★★	★★★	★★★	★★★
Summarizing	★★	★★	★★★	★★
Teaching others	★★	★★★	★★	★★★
Using writing frames	★★★	★★★	★★	★★
Key	★ **Less than ideal**		★★ **Suitable**	★★★ **Ideal**

Engagement Routines by Quadrant

Some examples of structured engagement routines are rated for their appropriateness to each quadrant below.

Routine	Quadrant A Acquisition	Quadrant B Application	Quadrant C Assimilation	Quadrant D Adaptation
Answers Up	★	★	★	★
Choral Responses	★★	★★	★	★
Give One—Get One	★★★	★★★	★★	★★
Idea Wave	★★★	★★★	★★	★★
Inquiry	★	★★	★★★	★★★
Jigsaw Groups	★	★★	★★★	★★★
Numbered Heads	★	★	★	★
Partner and Group Interactions	★★	★★★	★★	★★★
Pick and Point	★★★	★★★	★	★
Purposeful Viewing	★★★	★★	★★	★★
Question Chains	★★	★★	★★★	★★★
Setting Up and Monitoring Tasks	★★★	★★★	★★	★★
Show of Thumbs	★★★	★★★	★	★
Socratic Seminar	★	★	★★★	★★★
Think-(Write)-Pair-Share	★★★	★★★	★★	★★
Thumbs Up/Thumbs Down	★★★	★★★	★	★
Turn and Talk	★★★	★★★	★★	★★
Using Response Frames	★★★	★★★	★★	★★
Write and Reveal	★★★	★★★	★★	★★
Key	★ Less than ideal	★★ Suitable	★★★ Ideal	

Student Work Products by Quadrant

Reflecting on the student work through the products that are included in the activity is one way to identify and raise the current levels of rigor and relevance.

Demonstrating Learning

Consider the context and work that students are engaged in when determining the level of rigor and relevance. The following is a list of student work products linked to each quadrant of the Rigor/Relevance Framework. Your students can use these work products to demonstrate learning in each quadrant.

- Some student work products can be used in multiple quadrants.
- Products are listed where they are most frequently used.

Quadrant C	
• Abstract	• Exhibit
• Annotation	• Inventory
• Blog	• Investigation
• Chart	• Journal
• Classification	• Outline

Quadrant D	
• Adaptation	• Newspaper
• Blueprint	• Play
• Book	• Poem
• Brochure	• Song
• Debate	• Trial
• Device	• Video
• Editorial	

Quadrant A	
• Answer	• Reproduction
• Definition	• Selection
• Explanation	• True/False
• List	• Worksheet
• Quiz	
• Recitation	

Quadrant B	
• Collage	• Performance
• Collection	• Service
• Data	• Skit
• Demonstration	• Solution
• Interpretation	• Survey

Teacher Question Stems by Quadrant

In your learning environment, try using the following question stems that align to each quadrant. This can help move students toward increased rigor and relevance.

C	D
Ask questions to summarize, analyze, organize, or evaluate:	**Ask questions to predict, design, or create:**
• How are these similar/different? • How is the main idea supported by key details in the text? • What's another way we could say/explain/express that? • What do you think are some of the reasons/causes that _____? • Why did _____ changes occur? • How can you distinguish between _____? • What is a better solution to _____? • How would you defend your position about _____? • What changes to _____ would you recommend? • What evidence from the resources support your thinking? • Where in the text is that explicit? • Which ones do you think belong together? • What things/events lead up to _____?	• How would you design a _____ to _____? • How would you rewrite the ending to the story? • What would be different today if that event occurred as _____? • Can you see a possible solution to _____? • How could you teach that to others? • If you had access to all the resources, how would you deal with _____? • How would you devise your own way to deal with _____? • What new and unusual uses would you create for _____? • Can you develop a proposal that would _____? • How would you have handled _____? • How would you do it differently? • How does the text support your argument? • Can you describe your reasoning?

Teacher Question Stems by Quadrant (*continued*)

Ask questions to recall facts, make observations, or demonstrate understanding:	Ask questions to apply or relate:
• What is/are _____ ? • How many _____ ? • How do/does _____ ? • What did you observe _____ ? • What else can you tell me about _____ ? • What does it mean to _____ ? • What can you recall about _____ ? • Where did you find that _____ ? • Who is/was _____ ? • In what ways _____ ? • How would you define that in your own terms? • What do/did you notice about this _____ ? • What do/did you feel/hear/see/smell _____ ? • What do/did you remember about _____ ? • What did you find out about _____ ?	• How would you do that? • Where will you use that knowledge? • How does that relate to your experience? • How can you demonstrate that? • What observations relate to _____ ? • Where would you locate that information? • Can you calculate that for _____ ? • How would you illustrate that? • How would you interpret that? • Who could you interview? • How would you collect that data? • How do you know it works? • Can you show me? • Can you apply what you know to this real-world problem? • How do you make sure it is done correctly?
A	B

Technology Use by Quadrant

Empower students to consider the following examples of technology use by quadrant.

Quadrant C	
• Editing	• Reverse
• Hyperlinking	engineering
• Media clipping/	• Software
cropping	cracking
• Monitoring	• Testing
• Photos/video	• Validating
• Programming	resources

Quadrant D	
• Animating	• Mashing-mixing/
• Audio casting	remixing
• Blog comments	• Networking
• Broadcasting	• Photo/video
• Collaborating	blogging
• Composing	• Podcasting
• Digital	• Reviewing
storytelling	
• Directing	

Quadrant A	
• Bullets and lists	• Internet
• Creating and	searching
naming folders	• Loading
• Editing	• Typing
• Highlight-	• Using a
selecting	mouse
	• Word doc

Quadrant B	
• Advanced	• Replying—
searching	commenting
• Annotating	• Sharing
• Blogs	• Social bookmarking
• Google Docs	• Subscribing to RSS
• Operating/	feed
running a	• Tagging
program	• Texting
• Posting—social	• Uploading
media	• Web authoring

Data Team Assessment Cycle Example

Monday	Tuesday	Wednesday	Thursday	Friday
30 Unit 1: Buffer Week (Unit 1 *Post-Assessment* & Data Team Meeting previous week)	1 Unit 2: *Pre-Assessment*	2	3 **Data Team Meeting** 5 Steps, Unit 2	4
7 Unit 2 Begins	8	9	10 **Data Team Meeting** Monitoring	11
14	15	16	17 **Data Team Meeting** Monitoring	18
21	22 Short-Cycle *Mid-Assessment*	23	24 **Data Team Meeting** 5 Steps, Unit 2	25
28	29	30	31 **Data Team Meeting** Monitoring	1
4	5	6 Unit 2: *Post-Assessment*	7 **Data Team Meeting** 5 Steps Unit 2: Post-Assessment	8 Unit 2: Buffer Week
11 Unit 2: Buffer Week continues Unit 3: *Pre-Assessment*	12	13 **Data Team Meeting** 5 Steps, Unit 3	14	15 Unit 3 Begins

Data Teams Implementation Rubric

		Process		
Step 1		**Proficient**	**Exemplary** (All Proficient Criteria, Plus:)	**Comments**
	COLLECT AND CHART DATA	Formative assessments are administered prior to the start of instruction to allow for data-based planning.	Formative assessments have identified success criteria aligned to the learning progression (scoring guides).	
		Data is assembled in discussion format prior to the start of the meeting.	Results are disaggregated according to specific subgroups.	
		Data collection includes the number and names of students at different levels of performance.	All team members, including support personnel who may not be able to attend the meeting, have access to the results.	
		Data is disaggregated by the teacher.		
		Formative assessment is aligned to the Priority Standard. The standard is "unwrapped," and Webb's Depth of Knowledge(DOK) levels are identified.		
		The Data Team meets within three days of the administration of the formative assessment in order to analyze results.		

Notes and Observations for Step 1:

Data Teams Implementation Rubric

	Proficient	Exemplary (All Proficient Criteria, Plus:)	Comments
Step 2			
ANALYZE AND PRIORITIZE	The inferring of strengths and needs is based on a direct analysis of student work.	Prioritized needs reflect areas that will have impact within multiple skill areas.	
	Strengths and needs are identified for each performance group.	Needs inferred for the intervention groups are aligned to the learning progression of the standard.	
	Identified strengths and needs are within the direct influence of teachers.		
	The team goes beyond labeling the need, or the "what," to infer the root cause, or the "why."		
	Needs are prioritized to reflect those areas that will have the greatest impact on the Priority Standard/ learning progression.		

Notes and Observations for Step 2:

Data Teams Implementation Rubric

		Process (continued)	
Step 3		**Proficient**	**Exemplary** (All Proficient Criteria, Plus:)	**Comments**
SMART GOAL		The team establishes, reviews, or revises the instructional goal.	The goal will have impact in multiple skill areas.	
		The team writes goals specific to the subject area and grade level, and student groups are identified.	Intervention students have a goal related to the prerequisite skills/learning progression necessary for proficiency.	
		A measurable area of need is established and the assessment to be used is identified.		
		Achievable gains in student learning are determined based on the current performance of all students.		
		The team focuses on relevant goals that address urgent areas that meet or exceed the SMART goals of the School Improvement Plan.		

Notes and Observations for Step 3:

Data Teams Implementation Rubric

	Proficient	Exemplary (All Proficient Criteria, Plus:)	Comments
Process (continued)			
Step 4			
SELECT STRATEGIES	Team members select strategies that directly target the prioritized needs identified during their analysis.	The strategies selected impact multiple skill areas.	
	The strategies describe the actions of adults that change the cognition of students.	Teachers model how the selected strategies are implemented to ensure consistency and efficacy.	
	The team agrees on prioritized research-based strategies that will have the greatest impact.	The team evaluates its capacity to use the selected instructional strategies and identifies needed resources, etc.	
	The descriptions of the strategies are specific enough to allow for replication.		
	The team describes specific and differentiated strategies for each performance group.		

Notes and Observations for Step 4:

Data Teams Implementation Rubric

	Process (continued)		
Step 5	**Proficient**	**Exemplary (All Proficient Criteria, Plus:)**	**Comments**
DETERMINE RESULTS INDICATORS	Results indicators are created for each selected strategy.	The team establishes an interim time frame to monitor the implementation of the strategy.	
	The team describes specifically what each educator will be doing to ensure the selected strategies are implemented with fidelity.	Indicators contain clear and detailed descriptions that allow others to replicate the described practices.	
	Indicators describe what the students will be doing as they are engaged with the strategy.	Students use success criteria from the learning progression to assess their own learning.	
	The team describes the anticipated, immediate changes in student work that will indicate the strategy is having the desired impact on learning.		

Notes and Observations for Step 5:

References

Ainsworth, Larry. 2003. *"Unwrapping" the Standards: A Simple Process to Make Standards Manageable.* Denver, CO: Advanced Learning Press.

Ainsworth, Larry, and Kyra Donovan. 2019. *Rigorous Curriculum Design.* Rexford, NY: International Center for Leadership in Education.

Anderson, Lorin W., and David R. Krathwohl. 2001. *A Taxonomy for Learning, Teaching, and Assessing: A Revision of Bloom's Taxonomy of Educational Objectives.* New York: Longman.

Association for Supervision and Curriculum Development (ASCD). 2020. "Common Core Standards Adoption by State." Retrieved October 15, 2020. http://www.ascd.org/common-core-state-standards/common-core-state-standards-adoption-map.aspx.

Bambrick-Santoyo, P. 2019. *Driven by Data 2.0.* San Francisco, CA: Jossey-Bass/Wiley.

Clark, Timothy R. 2020. *The 4 Stages of Psychological Safety.* Oakland, CA: Berrett-Koehler.

Common Core State Standards Initiative. 2020. http://www.corestandards.org/.

Csikszentmihalyi, Mihaly. 1996. *Creativity: Flow and the Psychology of Discovery and Invention.* New York: HarperCollins.

Donohoo, Jenni. 2017. *Collective Efficacy.* Thousand Oaks, CA: Corwin.

Donohoo, Jenni, John Hattie, and Rachel Eells. 2018. "The Power of Collective Efficacy." *Educational Leadership*, March 28, 2018, p. 40–44.

Donohoo, Jenni, and Moses Velasco. 2016. *The Transformative Power of Collaborative Inquiry.* Thousand Oaks, CA: Corwin.

Drummond, Adam. 2019. *The Instructional Change Agent.* Rexford, NY: International Center for Leadership in Education.

DuFour, Richard. 2010. "Why Educators Should Be Given Time to Collaborate." *Education Week* 30 (9): 15.

DuFour, Richard, and Robert Eaker. 1998. *Professional Learning Communities at Work: Best Practices for Enhancing Student Achievement.* Bloomington, IN: Solution Tree.

Dweck, Carol. 2017. *Mindset: The New Psychology of Success*, updated edition. New York: Ballantine Books.

Firestone, Allison, Rebecca Cruz, and Janelle Rodl. 2020. "Teacher Study Groups: An Integrative Literature Synthesis." *Review of Education Research* 90 (5): 675–709.

Fisher, Douglas, Nancy Frey, John Almarode, Karen Flories, and Dave Nagel. 2020. *The PLC+ Playbook*. Thousand Oaks, CA: Corwin.

Fisher, Douglas, Nancy Frey, and Dominique Smith. 2020. *The Teacher Credibility and Collective Efficacy Playbook*. Thousand Oaks, CA: Corwin.

Graves, Michael. 2005. *The Vocabulary Book: Learning and Instruction*. Urbana, IL: National Council of Teachers of English.

Hattie, John. *Visible Learning for Teachers*. 2012. New York: Routledge.

Hattie, John. 2017. "Misinterpreting the Growth Mindset: Why We're Doing Students a Disservice." *Finding Common Ground* blog. Retrieved October 31, 2020. https://blogs.edweek.org/edweek/finding_common_ground/2017/06/misinterpreting_the_growth_mindset_why_were_doing_students_a_disservice.html.

Hattie, John, and Raymond Smith, eds. 2021. *Ten Mindframes for Leaders*. Thousand Oaks, CA: Corwin.

Hattie, John, and Klaus Zierer. 2018. *10 Mindframes for Visible Learning*. New York: Routledge.

Hattie, John, and Klaus Zierer. 2019. *Visible Learning Insights*. New York: Routledge.

Hoff, David J. 2001. "'New Standards' Leaves Legacy of Unmet Goals." *Education Week*, August 8, 2001. Retrieved October 15, 2020. https://www.edweek.org/ew/articles/2001/08/08/43standards.h20.html.

Jensen, Eric. 2013. *Engaging Students with Poverty in Mind*. Alexandria, VA: Association for Curriculum and Staff Development, p. 70.

Johansen, Bob. 2012. *Leaders Make the Future*. Oakland, CA: Berrett-Koehler.

Kieschnick, Weston, and Molly Kieschnick. 2020. *Breaking Bold*. Rexford, NY: International Center for Leadership in Education.

Lambert, Bernadette. 2016. *Moving Beyond Quadrant A: Developing Rigor, Relevance, and Learner Engagement in Your Classroom*. Rexford, NY: International Center for Leadership in Education, p. 11.

Marzano, Robert J. 2004. *Building Background Knowledge for Academic Achievement: Research on What Works in Schools*. Alexandria, VA: Association for Curriculum and Staff Development.

MPR News Staff. 2020. "MPR Says DJ Eric Malmberg Fired from The Current," *Morning Edition*. Retrieved September 15, 2020. https://www.mprnews.org/story/2020/09/14/mpr-president-duchesne-drew-on-marianne-combs-resignation.

Murray, Thomas C. 2019. *Personal and Authentic: Designing Learning Experiences That Impact a Lifetime*. IM Press.

National Governors Association Center for Best Practices, Council of Chief State School Officers. 2010. *Common Core State Standards for English Language Arts and Literacy in History/Social Studies, Science, and Technical Subjects*. Washington, DC: National Governors Association Center for Best Practices, Council of Chief State School Officers.

Palmer, Parker. 1983. *To Know and Be Known*. New York: Harper Collins.

Pate, Alexs. 2020. *The Innocent Classroom: Dismantling Racial Bias to Support Students of Color*. Alexandria, VA: Association for Curriculum and Staff Development.

Power, Karen. 2020. "Lessons Learned This September." *School Improvement Blog,* October 2, 2020. Retrieved October 3, 2020. https://karenpower .blog/2020/10/03/lessons-learned-this-september/.

Reeves, Douglas B., and Tony Flach. 2011. "Meaningful Analysis Can Rescue Schools from Drowning in Data," *Leaning Forward,* August, Vol. 32 No. 4. https://static1.squarespace.com/static/56a6ae1c22482e2f99869834/t/5790c071 3e00bebc2bde35bf/1469104242508/Data+.pdf

Schmoker, Michael. 2005. "No Turning Back: The Ironclad Case for Professional Learning Communities." In *On Common Ground: The Power of Professional Learning Communities,* edited by R. DuFour, R. Eaker, and R. DuFour, 135–154. Bloomington, IN: Solution Tree Press, p. 135.

Schmoker, Michael J. 2006. *Results Now: How We Can Achieve Unprecedented Improvements in Teaching and Learning.* Alexandria, VA: ASCD, p. 177.

Schwandt, Thomas A. 1989. "Solutions to the Paradigm Conflict: Coping with Uncertainty." *Journal of Contemporary Ethnography* 17 (4): 379–407.

Sinek, Simon. 2011. *Start with Why.* New York: Penguin.

Sinek, Simon. 2016. *Together Is Better.* New York: Penguin, pp. 42, 105.

Sparks, Sarah. 2013. "Social-Emotional Needs Entwined with Students' Learning, Security." *Education Week,* January 4, 2013. Retrieved October 15, 2020. https:// www.edweek.org/ew/articles/2013/01/10/16environment.h32.html.

Trei, Lisa. 2007. "Fixed Versus Growth Intelligence Mindsets." Stanford News Service. February 7, 2007. Retrieved June 8, 2020. https://news.stanford.edu/ pr/2007/pr-dweck-020707.html.

Tuckman, Bruce W. 1965. "Developmental Sequence in Small Groups." *Psychological Bulletin* 63 (6): 384–399. doi:10.1037/h0022100. PMID 14314073.

Tyler, Ralph W. 1949. *Basic Principles of Curriculum and Instruction.* Chicago: University of Chicago Press.

Venables, Daniel. 2014. *Data into Action.* Alexandria, VA: Association for Curriculum and Staff Development.

Webb, N. 2005. "Depth-of-Knowledge Levels for Four Content Areas." Presentation to the Florida Education Research Association, 50th Annual Meeting, November, 2005, Miami, Florida.

Wiggins, Grant. 2012. "Seven Keys to Effective Feedback." *Educational Leadership* 70 (1): 10–16. Retrieved October 15, 2020. http://www.ascd.org/publications/ educational-leadership/sept12/vol70/num01/Seven-Keys-to-Effective-Feedback.aspx.